BIRDS *of*
INDIANAPOLIS

BIRDS *of*

INDIANAPOLIS

A GUIDE TO THE REGION

*by Charles E. Keller and
Timothy C. Keller*

INDIANA UNIVERSITY PRESS
Bloomington • Indianapolis

The paper used in this publication meets the minimum requirements of American National Standard for Information Sciences—Permanence of Paper for Printed Library Materials, ANSI Z39.48-1984.

Manufactured in the United States of America

Library of Congress Cataloging-in-Publication Data
Keller, Charles E., date.
    Birds of Indianapolis : a guide to the region / by Charles E. Keller and Timothy C. Keller.
        p.   cm.
    Includes bibliographical references and index.
    ISBN 0-253-33119-6 (cloth). — ISBN 0-253-28534-8 (paper)
    1. Birds—Indiana—Indianapolis.   2. Bird watching—Indiana—Indianapolis—Guidebooks.   I. Keller, Timothy C., date.
II. Title.
QL684.I5K43   1993
598'.072347725—dc20   92-46532

1 2 3 4 5   97 96 95 94 93

To the memory of
John W. and Lucille J. Keller
parents and grandparents of the authors
They understood

Contents

Illustrations follow page 20.

Acknowledgments

Both of us have benefited from the numerous observers and field acquaintances that we have known over the years. We also owe a special debt of gratitude to John Gallman, Patricia Newforth, and Roberta Diehl of Indiana University Press for their interest and helpful suggestions.

BIRDS *of*

INDIANAPOLIS

The increasing popularity of birdwatching, or birding as it is more often known today, can be attested to by the many people who go on Audubon Society-sponsored field trips,

INTRO-DUCTION

have feeding stations in their yards, or simply express curiosity about one of nature's more interesting phenomena. One reason may be that there is more available recreational free time, and another surely is the increasing concern about the environment in general.

But we tend to think that a growing awareness of birds' aesthetic beauty and fascination with the mystery of their habits also play a large part in this upsurge. Who has not thrilled at the sight of a hunting Peregrine Falcon or the aerial gyrations of a flock of shorebirds? What about the majesty of trumpeting Sandhill Cranes or the flight of wild geese? Even the most casual observer, suddenly noticing the first robin in spring or an unidentified bird at the feeder, sooner or later wants to learn more about these fascinating creatures.

In our combined eighty years of photographing, banding, and watching birds in Indianapolis, we've also chalked up much experience in observing birders. The vast majority of birders, we've noticed, tend to shy away from the more "technical" information that is available. It is to assist this large segment of the Indianapolis birding community that we present a concise selection of birds that average citizens of our fair city are liable to see from their yards or on occasional trips to parks of the region. (For purposes of this book, Indianapolis is defined as all of Marion County plus the surrounding counties of Boone, Hamilton, Hancock, Hendricks, Johnson, Morgan, and Shelby.)

When we chose the 125 birds (96 of which are shown in color photographs) to write about for this book, we admittedly showed some bias. By and large, they are all species that frequent our city parks or backyards. A few can be found near rivers, lakes, and ponds, or in fields and surrounding woodlots. But we could not resist including a few of our favorite rarities. However, all are species that the casual observer has a good chance of seeing in central Indiana.

For more serious birders, a complete listing of the 341 species of birds seen in or attributed to the region is included in a checklist at the end of this book. If you like to keep lists, there is a place to check off those species which you have observed.

We have listed the birds we write about here the same way they are listed in most field identification guides—in taxonomic order, from least to most evolved species, as established by the American Ornithologists' Union—rather than using some other rationale for organization (e.g., habitat, color, alphabetical order, etc.). In other respects we have stayed away from the field guide approach. There is a plethora of such information already available and no need to duplicate the fine works now on the market (see "Birdwatching Aids").

ATTRACTING BIRDS

Encouraging birds to visit your yard is not only an enjoyable pastime but can also be very informative. Indeed, amateurs have contributed a great deal to scientific knowledge by studying bird behavior at feeding stations. To name one instance, the pathbreaking life history of the Song Sparrow was written in the 1930s near Columbus, Ohio, by a housewife who was not a trained scientist but rather a talented observer.

Whether you are a photographer who likes to get good shots of birds and other animals or just someone who enjoys watching them at close range, having your own feeding station and backyard wildlife sanctuary will provide ample opportunity. As a fringe benefit, you may get some fairly unusual visitors. We personally know of a couple who even attract wild foxes to their yard, well within the city limits.

Entire books have been written on the subject of gardening to attract wildlife in general and birds in particular. We will simply say that plants native to the Midwest do a better job of attracting native species of birds than alien ornamentals from, for example, Japan or Eastern Europe, as well as being more disease- and trouble-free. Natives like wild cherry, honeysuckle, trumpet vines, crabapple, sunflowers, flowering dogwoods, and even the sycamore attract a wide variety of wildlife. Other good things to do include leaving piles of brush and dead trees alone whenever possible (to provide shelter) and having some source of water for drinking and bathing.

Feeding trays and other types of feeders should be placed so that birds using them will have some cover nearby. Ideally they should be mounted next to a large bush or shrub, preferably near a picture window or some other convenient vantage point. A variety of feeds are available, but in our experience the best all-around attractant is oil sunflower seeds.

For American Goldfinches and House Finches we suggest thistle seed placed in the long cylindrical tubes that can be found at any hardware or feed store.

In late spring and through the summer, hummingbird feeders filled with a one-to-four ratio of sugar to water will attract hummers. Boil equal parts of sugar and water and then dilute the mixture according to the above ratio.

Putting out suet in wire enclosures will attract woodpeckers, nuthatches, creepers, kinglets, and other fat-loving species.

Don't forget to scatter cracked corn and other seed on the ground for ground-feeding species like Northern Bobwhite, American Tree Sparrows, Dark-eyed Juncos, etc.

Birdbaths (faithfully kept clean and filled) make a necessary addition to a well-stocked feeding area and will often attract a wide variety of birds, particularly warblers during the fall migration.

For detailed information on landscaping, building bird houses, and feeding we recommend Stephen W. Kress's fine reference, *The Audubon Society Guide to Attracting Birds* (Scribner, 1985).

GETTING STARTED BIRDWATCHING

There is no better way for the novice to get started birdwatching than to become involved with a group that conducts regular field trips. In Indianapolis, bird hikes are held every Sunday morning at Eagle Creek Park and, from September to May, in other locations by the Amos W. Butler Audubon Society, a branch of the National Audubon Society (phone: 317-926-9456).

When in the field it is important not only to dress appropriately but to wear comfortable shoes. Also, carry a pair of binoculars and at least one field guide.

While you are with a group be sure to show consideration for the leader by staying back, being relatively quiet, and watching and listening attentively. Many times there will be other expert birders along who can give you identification hints. Children are always welcome, but pets usually are inappropriate, as they may tend to frighten waterfowl and shorebirds.

On your first field trip, you may notice that the leader makes strange sounds from time to time. These sounds are used to entice a number of the tamer and more curious birds into view for a better look; one, which birders call "pishing," is a quick series of sibilant hisses or pssst's. (When we mention "pishing" in the text in connection with one species or another, this is what we mean—it is *not* a typographical error.) Another useful sound is a series of squeaky kisses on the back of one's hand. They are valuable tricks to learn but should be heard, as they are difficult to describe.

What season of the year is best to begin birding? Winter, believe it or not. At that time the leaves are off the trees and the number of species that can be seen is not overwhelming. In late December local Christmas Counts are held with the idea not only of promoting sociable companionship, but of trying to see as many species as possible within a fifteen-mile radius of a central point. Later, in January or early February, one can usually count on seeing between twenty-five and thirty species during any one outing.

Numbers of species and individual birds begin to swell in early March with the onset of waterfowl migration. By early to mid-May the spring migration has reached its peak, and the woods and fields are often alive with a myriad variety of species.

During the summer months the local breeding birds are about, and in early July the first migrating shorebirds begin to appear on the mudflats of our lakes and streams.

By late August you can begin looking for the first returning warblers, and the first southbound hawks start to appear in September. The bulk of the waterfowl move through in late October and through November. There is no off-season for birding.

What time of day is best for birdwatching? Early in the morning is prime time, for that is when birds are hungry and begin actively singing and looking for food. Later during the heat of the day they become somewhat lethargic and harder to see. They become slightly more active once again just before dusk. So if you want to see the most birds, begin early in the morning.

Visit as wide a variety of habitats as possible. Lakes and streams are usually good for waterfowl and other aquatic birds. Old fields generally yield larks, sparrows, and the like, while deep woods are good for forest-loving species. It is at the field edges where the woods meet the open fields that the most species are generally found: cover affords protection, and there are opportunities to feed. If you are looking for shorebirds, rain-filled fields or the dried-up peripheries of lakes and reservoirs with resultant mudflats are usually good during May and from July through October.

During inclement weather in the spring and fall when stalled cold fronts dam up migrating birds, they often are seen in a wider variety of habitats. Birders love these so-called migrant traps, in which rare species can be found with a minimum of effort.

LISTING

As you progress in your birding expertise you will probably want to start listing the birds you see. Your listing can be as detailed as you wish, but we would suggest that, if you take your birding seriously and wish to contribute potentially valuable data over the ensuing years, you record not only the species seen but numbers as well. By doing so you can furnish needed information about population dynamics—whether a certain species or group of species is increasing or decreasing over the years. Has our environment changed, or is it beginning to change? You may even wish to personalize your lists by making notations about the weather, any unusual behavior observed, the number of observers, and other pertinent data.

If you should have the good fortune to spot a rare species and you want your observation to be believed, then by all means document it by means of detailed notes or, better still, by photographing the bird. Both the first Brambling and the first House Finch seen in the Indianapolis area were documented by photographs. A wayward Trumpeter Swan was even captured on film by Bill Brink at Eagle Creek Reservoir.

Listing is a contagious sport, and one that can be expanded to encompass other states, local areas, and even your own backyard. Greg Oskay, who lives on the south side, has identified some eighty-three species during a twelve-year period from his well-landscaped backyard. We think you'll find listing fun and suggest you try it.

BIRDWATCHING AIDS

One of the most common mistakes of beginning birders is choosing the wrong binoculars. Bigger is not better. Too often we have seen birders struggling with binoculars that are too heavy for general use. (A binocular weighing more than thirty ounces can feel like a mill-stone around your neck by the end of a rigorous birding trip.) Or they buy binoculars that are too powerful, so that the slightest breath or movement makes steady observation nearly impossible. Long, dangling neck straps are another mistake. They are to blame for many a binocular broken while climbing a fence or fording a small stream. As for zoom eyepieces, they severely limit your field of view (the diameter of the viewing area) and correspondingly decrease the amount of light transmitted to the eye.

There are a number of very fine binoculars on the market, and not all of them are expensive. The ideal binocular is easy to handle, light in weight, close focusing, optically sharp, and above all one that you feel comfortable with. For birding we recommend 7×35, 8×30, or 10×50. The first figure indicates the number of times the object is magnified, while the latter figure refers to relative brightness. For eye-glass wearers there are binoculars that have roll-down eyecups and what is termed a large exit pupil. The larger the exit pupil, the better. We suggest that you keep trying different brands and models until you find the pair that's right for you.

If you live near a reservoir, lake, or open area, a spotting scope can be a definite asset. Be sure to choose a tripod for your scope that is sturdy and easy to set up. Good spotting scopes come with a variety of eyepieces ranging from fixed to zoom.

As important as the correct optical equipment is the choice of a field guide. Today there are a number of fine field guides on the market, including the National Geographic Society's *Field Guide to the Birds of North America* and the famous "Peterson Guide," formally known as *A Field Guide to the Birds (East of the Rockies)* (Houghton Mifflin Co., 1980). They can be purchased at bird specialty stores, and the latter is also available at most book stores. For other references see "Suggestions for Further Reading."

GREATER INDIANAPOLIS AND AREA

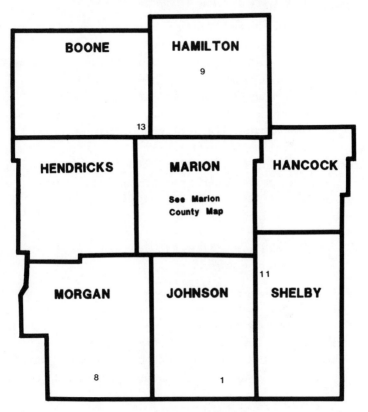

FINDING BIRDS IN THE INDIANAPOLIS REGION

The city of Indianapolis is surrounded by good birding spots. Below is a sampling of those which we consider among the more important, with instructions on how to get there. (The numbers are keyed to the maps.) There are also numerous city parks in metropolitan Indianapolis that sometimes offer fair viewing of some of the more common species.

When rare birds are spotted anywhere in the state, including the area covered by this book, they are usually reported on the Indiana Audubon Society Hotline (317-259-0911). If planning a birdwatching excursion, you may wish to phone the hotline before finalizing your destination.

[1] *Atterbury Fish and Wildlife Area*

The Atterbury Fish and Wildlife Area is about five miles south of Franklin, in Johnson County. To reach it travel south on U.S. 31 to State Road 252. Drive west on 252 about two miles to the road marked Johnson County Park (School House Road). Turn left on this road and proceed about 2 miles to the entrance. A map can be obtained from the headquarters building, just north of the Burnside and Hospital Road junction. The area is good habitat for grassland and secondary growth species, including Sedge Wren, Dickcissel, Grasshopper and Henslow's Sparrow, Blue Grosbeak, Orchard Oriole, and Bobolink. The rare Tricolored Heron, Greater White-fronted Goose, Eurasian Wigeon, American Avocet, and Bachman's Sparrow have also been spotted there.

[2] *Butler University Canal Towpath and Holcomb Gardens*

The Butler University Canal Towpath and Holcomb Gardens border White River in northern Indianapolis. They are located off West 46th Street. Enter the university grounds and proceed north via the road that parallels Holcomb Observatory. Go past the observatory and down the hill toward the canal. The large woods is a good place to warbler watch during May and again in September and October.

[3] *Eagle Creek Reservoir and Park*

Perhaps the prime birding spot in the entire city is Eagle Creek Reservoir and Park, between 56th Street and 71st Street off I-465 on the northwest side of Indianapolis. Fair numbers of waterfowl occur there in March and April and again in October and November. During the fall when the water level has receded, the mudflats at the north end of the reservoir can have an impressive shorebird migration. Warbler watching is good in May and again in September in the

MARION COUNTY (INDIANAPOLIS)

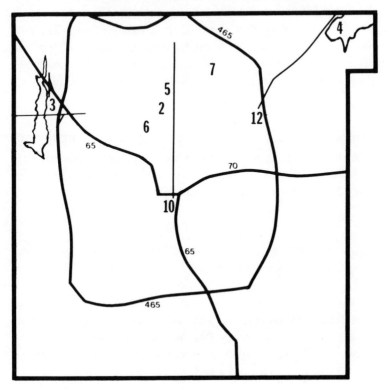

vicinity of the nature center, which has an air-conditioned viewing room overlooking the reservoir and a hummingbird garden. Feeders nearby often host a variety of other species. A group of about thirty Turkey Vultures roost near the waterfowl resting area just behind the center. In the eastern part of the park there are three small ponds off Reed Road which can be good for waterfowl, rails, and other marsh-loving species. Some of the rarities recorded at Eagle Creek include American White Pelican, Trumpeter Swan, Mississippi Kite, American Avocet, Hudsonian and Marbled Godwit, and Black-legged Kitti-wake. There have been many others. Bird hikes led by local experts are conducted each Sunday. Call the Eagle Creek nature center (317-291-5618) for more information. There is an entrance fee to the park and nature center, and maps are available.

[4] *Geist Reservoir*

Geist Reservoir is located northeast of Indianapolis south of Fall Creek Road. To reach it drive on I-465 to the Shadeland Avenue exit to Fall Creek Road. Follow this road approximately four miles. Various other roads circle the reservoir. Unfortunately, the birding is now rather restricted because of real estate development. The north end of the reservoir is often attractive during the fall for shorebirds.

[5] *Holliday Park*

Holliday Park, just southeast of 64th Street and Spring Mill Road in northern Indianapolis, is in the process of being redeveloped after a number of years in disrepair. Here a series of park trails border White River that can be attractive to migrating birds.

[6] *Indianapolis Museum of Art*

The well-landscaped grounds of the Indianapolis Museum of Art, located at the northwest corner of Michigan Road and 38th Street, are a good location for many migrating land birds and winter finches. The Amos W. Butler Audubon Society stocks the feeders by the horticultural greenhouses near the east entrance. Here during some winters it may be possible to see Pine Siskins, Common Redpolls, and Evening Grosbeaks. A variety of other species frequent these feeders and can easily be seen from a parked car.

[7] *Marott Park*

Marott Park, at the corner of College Avenue and 73rd Street, also attracts migrating land birds. The park is traversed by Williams Creek and lies just north of White River.

[8] *Morgan-Monroe State Forest*

Morgan-Monroe State Forest is about two miles south of Martinsville. The area hosts nesting Pine Warblers, Worm-eating Warblers, and Hooded Warblers. Wild Turkeys and Ruffed Grouse are frequently seen early in the morning. A number of excellent trails traverse the area. A map can be obtained at the headquarters building, located some five miles from the west entrance inside the forest.

[9] *Morse Reservoir*

Morse Reservoir, about thirty miles north of Indianapolis and just north of the town of Noblesville, is fairly good for waterfowl during early spring and late fall. Access is sometimes difficult because of real estate development, but some vantage points exist at the dam and from the bridge that crosses the reservoir near the town of Cicero.

[10] *University Park*

Downtown, University Park, between Meridian and Pennsylvania streets and just south of Vermont Street, becomes a unique migrant trap during the fall migration, seemingly because of the tall buildings surrounding it. Night-flying birds are sometimes grounded here, especially when conditions are foggy or during heavy rain, and for several days this small one-block park may be alive with grounded migrants. Some of the species seen include Virginia Rail, Winter Wren, most of the warblers, and Clay-colored Sparrow. It is probably the best place to find Lincoln's Sparrow during late September and early October.

[11] *Walnut Grove*

Walnut Grove, a private campground and park, is located in Shelby County about five miles south of the I-74 London Road exit. It borders Sugar Creek, and there are numerous small sloughs and streams in the area. At one time it was prime habitat for Prothonotary Warblers, and Pileated Woodpeckers can still frequently be seen in the park itself. The flat fields to the east of Walnut Grove are frequented by Lapland Longspurs, Horned Larks, shorebirds during wet springs, and occasionally Snow Buntings.

[12] *Woollen's Gardens*

Woollen's Gardens lies in the northwest corner of the point where I-465 crosses Fall Creek on the east side of Indianapolis. Entrance is from Shadeland Avenue, which lies parallel to I-465. Unfortunately, the gardens are overgrown and not too well tended, but this can still be good warbler territory during the spring and fall migrations.

[13] *Starkey Park*

Starkey Park is located near Zionsville along the upper reaches of Eagle Creek in Boone County, and is one of the newer parks in our region. It is just now beginning to be explored ornithologically and appears to offer good habitat for a wide variety of passerine species.

We hope this book will stimulate you to explore the charming and interesting world of birdlife in the Indianapolis vicinity. We think you will find, as we have, that if you take the time, even a metropolitan area has much to offer the inquiring mind in the way of nature's wonders.

COMMON LOON

Gavia immer

Habitat: Large bodies of water, reservoirs, gravel pits.
Local Sites: All three nearby reservoirs, Eagle Creek, Geist, and Morse. Occasionally gravel and/or borrow pits.
Status: Fairly common spring migrant, appearing about 20 March and remaining until late April and sometimes into May. Very rare during the summer, when nonbreeding immature birds are sometimes seen. Fairly common to common fall migrant, 20 October to 1 December. Some birds will remain during the winter as long as there is open water. They nest north of us, in the more remote lakes of the northern United States and southern Canada.
Length: 32 inches.
Remarks: The Common Loon is the largest diving bird that can be seen in the Indianapolis area, where it most often occurs in its rather plain winter or juvenile plumage. The birds are normally silent while here, but we have occasionally heard them give a tremulous call during periods of inclement weather. At other times when loons are present in large numbers, as occasionally happens at Eagle Creek Reservoir during the fall, they give a similar call, generally prior to departure from the area.

Loons require a large water surface in order to become airborne; at Geist Reservoir during the winter we have noted individuals stranded on the ice, unable to launch themselves into the air. Such cases occur when there is a quick freeze, and unless the birds can reach open water, they soon perish.

Although loons are fairly primitive on the evolutionary scale and poorly adapted to a life on land, they have strongly webbed feet that enable them to swim with extraordinary facility. While watching birds in the waterfowl area behind the nature center at Eagle Creek Reservoir we have marveled at the length of time they can stay under water and the corresponding distances they cover, often returning to the surface far from their original point of submersion.

PIED-BILLED GREBE

Podilymbus podiceps

Habitat: Nests sparingly on small ponds or larger lakes with extensive marshy areas. During migration can occur almost anywhere there is water.

Local Sites: Eagle Creek, Geist, and Morse Reservoirs. During nesting season the ice-skating ponds at Eagle Creek Park may host a pair of breeding birds.

Status: Common migrant, arriving in the spring during March. Some rarely remain to breed in choice sites. During the fall birds begin appearing in late September and will often remain until December. They rarely winter and then only when water remains ice-free.

Length: $13^1/_2$ inches.

Remarks: Known to nineteenth-century birdwatchers as the Helldiver, the Pied-billed Grebe dives in search of crustaceans and invertebrates as well as fish for its sustenance. When frightened they frequently submerge so that only their heads are visible, one of the very few birds to do so. Strong swimmers, they can cover large distances underwater when threatened.

At Eagle Creek Park a pair nested at the ice-skating ponds during the summer of 1991. Here a nest of loosely constructed mounds of vegetation was built back amid the cattails and the young birds were occasionally seen riding on their mother's back. These young birds were attractive with their white, black, and red plumage, but these colors are lost with the first molt, when they become a nondescript brown.

Seldom flying except during migration, they are nevertheless strong fliers, traveling many hundreds of miles to and from their breeding areas and winter quarters. Their wingbeats are shallower and more rapid than those of most ducks. South of Indianapolis we have found dead grebes under high-tension wires which they no doubt hit while migrating during the night.

DOUBLE-CRESTED CORMORANT

Phalacrocorax auritus

Habitat: Occurs on large lakes and occasionally small ponds with extensive emergent brush or small islands upon which to perch.

Local Sites: Eagle Creek, Geist, and Morse Reservoirs and some of the larger gravel and/or borrow pits. Occasionally at Atterbury Fish and Wildlife Area.

Status: The species is in the act of rebounding from a disastrous period of years when pesticides decimated the population. It is now a rather uncommon migrant, appearing during March and remaining in some areas until early June. It returns in September and can often be found into December during mild winters. At present it does not nest in Indiana.

Length: 32 inches.

Remarks: Consummate fishermen, cormorants can be seen sunning themselves with wings spread wide in an effort to dry out before their next foray in the water. We have often seen them doing this on the islands in back of the nature center at Eagle Creek Reservoir during both the spring and fall migration periods.

Streamlined bodies and webbed feet make them excellent swimmers and divers. They sometimes fish as a group effort, herding fish into compact masses to make them easier to catch. Strong fliers, they form loose "V's" like geese or fly single file. Unlike geese, however, they can soar for some distance. Cormorants, as well as hawks and owls, cast pellets to get rid of unwanted fish bones and other undigestible parts of their prey.

GREAT BLUE HERON

Ardea herodias

Habitat: Reservoirs, ponds, and all types of waterways.

Local Sites: They feed at all three nearby reservoirs, Eagle Creek, Geist, and Morse, and nest in compact colonies of from twenty to over one hundred birds at locations near Geist and in northern Johnson County.

Status: Common migrant and fairly common nesting species, appearing during late February and remaining until the water freezes over; sometimes remaining through the winter during warm years.

Length: 46–54 inches with a wingspan up to 72 inches.

Remarks: To our minds there is nothing more majestic than a Great Blue Heron, or Blue Crane as it is often called, in flight. With neck drawn in tight against the body and slow ponderous wingbeats, it is the essence of stately grace.

One of the breeding sites near Geist Reservoir has managed to remain in use for at least thirty years in spite of nearby real estate development. Normally, however, Great Blue colonies are extremely vulnerable to disturbance and need large buffer zones. To protect such a region is for the benefit of everyone, particularly for future generations who deserve to marvel at this large and showy bird. On one occasion a former colony in Hendricks County was disturbed during the nesting season, and the understory and ground were cluttered with discarded or displaced sticks and dead young.

Although normally absent during the winter they occasionally can be seen at Geist and Eagle Creek Reservoirs, standing on thin sheet ice when caught by a sudden change in temperature.

GREAT EGRET

Casmerodius albus

Habitat: Reservoirs, ponds, and marshes.

Local Sites: All three nearby reservoirs, Eagle Creek, Geist, and Morse. Frequently found near fish hatcheries and small ponds and sometimes in Great Blue heronries, but not known to nest locally.

Status: Rare spring migrant, usually appearing in late April, and uncommon early summer (July) to early fall visitor when southern birds occur as they spread northward to favorite feeding areas.

Length: 39 inches with a wingspan of nearly 51 inches.

Remarks: When the water level is low during the early summer at some of our large reservoirs, this species often appears in what is termed post-breeding dispersal: adults and young birds wander away from their breeding areas farther south to places where competition for choice feeding sites may not be so keen.

In the early part of this century this species along with other members of the heron family was nearly exterminated by excess market hunting, particularly at the peak of the breeding season, when its long plumes or aigrettes were much sought after for milady's hat. Thanks to the efforts of the National Audubon Society, which set up breeding sanctuaries and championed protection, the Great Egret was spared so that succeeding generations could enjoy its beauty; however, the bird is still threatened in Florida by overdevelopment and in some other southern states by disturbance at nest sites and the lack of sufficient ground water reserves.

GREEN-BACKED HERON

Butorides striatus

Habitat: Inhabits a wider variety of habitat than the larger herons; found on virtually every waterway, stream, river, pond, lake, and reservoir. Nests are usually built in dense tangles of vines, bushes, or small trees.
Local Sites: All three nearby reservoirs, Eagle Creek, Geist, and Morse, as well as small streams, creeks, White River, and ponds.
Status: Fairly common resident, arriving about mid-April and remaining until late October. Occasionally a bird may winter where the water is ice-free and cover is adequate.
Length: 18 inches with a wingspan of 26 inches.
Remarks: The Green-backed Heron (or Fly-up-the-creek, as it was formerly called) is a familiar bird in the Indianapolis area. It seems to like the dense cover of the periphery of some of our smaller ponds, where it can often be seen stalking its prey. At such times the bird is poetry in slow motion as it places one foot in front of the other and extends its neck in anticipation of a quick strike to impale some unsuspecting prey. At other times birds have been noted twitching their tails and erecting their crests, especially when excited or just after

alighting from being flushed, but normally we see one with its head tucked in against its body, looking rather like a small stump.

Arthur Cleveland Bent in his classic and still useful Life History series relates that the old names of Chalk-line and Shite-poke express the commonly observed physiological effect of fright when the bird flushes, presumably serving the useful purpose of blinding a stealthily creeping pursuer.

BLACK-CROWNED NIGHT-HERON

Nycticorax nycticorax

Habitat: Waterways bounded by dense vegetation.
Local Sites: All three nearby reservoirs, Eagle Creek, Geist, and Morse. Occasionally found on small ponds and along river and stream waterways.
Status: Rare migrant; formerly nested. Appears during April, with some birds being seen in May. Post-breeding birds occur during late July and remain until October. Formerly wintered, but is not known to do so now.
Length: 25 inches with a 44-inch wingspan.
Remarks: The story of the disappearance of the Black-crowned Night-Heron as a breeding bird in the Indianapolis area is a chronicle of the environmental changes that have taken place here and in the state as a whole. Back in the early 1950s a breeding colony was located adjacent to White River just south of 30th Street and in back of the Veterans' Administration Hospital. Here a small colony of the birds set up housekeeping in a group of conifers that bordered the west side of White River Parkway. Birders and other interested observers could watch the breeding birds with comparative ease. Over the ensuing years the colony dwindled and the birds became increasingly rare in the area. Today, unfortunately, they cannot be found breeding anywhere in central Indiana. Herons, and particularly the Black-crowned, are at the top of a complex food chain and thus especially vulnerable to pesticides. It is open to question whether we will ever see this species return to this area as a breeding bird.

The adult Black-crowned is a handsome bird with striking black and white plumage and a brilliant red iris. The young bird takes about three years to attain full adult plumage and in the meantime is often confused with the American Bittern. It has a mosaic pattern of brown and white which makes the bird very difficult to see when it is at rest along the river bank. Like other members of the heron family, they seem to disperse after the breeding season, and can occasionally be found along our rivers and reservoirs.

They are more nocturnal than other herons, feeding mostly at dusk and into the evening hours and retreating into cover at dawn. Often the first indication of their presence is when the birds flush with a loud "Quak" as they depart. This heron has been declared an endangered species in the state and deserves protection.

TUNDRA SWAN

Cygnus columbianus

Habitat: Large bodies of water, reservoirs, and gravel pits.
Local Sites: All three nearby reservoirs, Eagle Creek, Geist, and Morse. Frequently seen at Atterbury Fish and Wildlife Area.
Status: Very rare migrant during the spring with the largest numbers being reported in November.
Length: 52 inches with a wingspan of about 80 inches.
Remarks: Although they are all large birds, this is the smallest and most delicate of the swans to be seen in central Indiana. Swans in general are stately birds; with their snow-white plumage and slow, graceful movements they appear quite regal.

Swans feed on aquatic vegetation by reaching down with their elongated necks to pluck plants from the lake bottom, occasionally tipping up like a duck to further extend their reach. In flight they can cover remarkable distances in a very short time; they have been clocked at over sixty miles per hour in the air. Their wingbeats are slow, deep, and powerful, giving them a look of unparalleled grace. When making long-distance flights they attain extremely high altitudes, up to 15,000 feet being reported in the literature.

Normally they migrate singly or in small flocks when passing through central Indiana; the largest flock in recent years consisted of nine birds at Eagle Creek Reservoir in December of 1991.

CANADA GOOSE

Branta canadensis

Habitat: Reservoirs, ponds, lakes, and streams.

Local Sites: The restocked version can be found just about anywhere there is sufficient water, but in particular Eagle Creek, Geist, and Morse Reservoirs and Atterbury Fish and Wildlife Area.

Status: Common migrant and nesting species. Restocked birds occur throughout most of the year, while the wild variety migrates through during late February to late March and once again in November and December.

Length: Ranges from 25 to 45 inches with wingspans of 50 to 76 inches, depending on race.

Remarks: A wide variety of subspecies of the Canada Goose are present in central Indiana, thanks to restocking efforts by government and private agencies. In some urban and suburban areas they have almost become pests, fouling ponds and lawns with their droppings and attacking small pets and children, although these encounters usually end without injury to either party.

During migration and on their winter feeding grounds they form immense flocks, often as many as ten thousand birds, and can become a problem for farmers: a flock this size can clean out a cornfield in very short order. It is an impressive spectacle—this many large birds in flight, their "V's" covering the sky and their honking calls deafening the ear.

The revenue that Canada Geese generate from hunters benefits other wildlife. Indiana's fish and wildlife areas are financed by hunting and fishing license fees, and national wildlife refuges are built and maintained though monies collected from duck stamp fees. These funds are used to construct and stock new wetland areas and to improve existing areas for wildlife propagation, providing habitat for all species even though they are created for game species such as the geese.

(Male birds or sex unknown unless otherwise stated)

Common Loon
(winter)

Pied-billed Grebe

Double-crested
Cormorant

Great Blue Heron

Great Egret

Green-backed Heron

Black-crowned
Night-Heron

Tundra Swan

Canada Goose

Wood Duck

Mallard
(male and female)

Blue-winged Teal
(male and female)

Canvasback

Lesser Scaup

Hooded Merganser

Turkey Vulture

Osprey

Bald Eagle

Northern Harrier

Cooper's Hawk
(female)

Red-tailed Hawk

American Kestrel
(female)

Wild Turkey

Sora

American Coot

Sandhill Crane

Killdeer

Lesser Yellowlegs

Spotted Sandpiper
(fall)

Upland Sandpiper

Semipalmated Sandpiper
(fall)

Pectoral Sandpiper

Common Snipe

Bonaparte's Gull
(fall)

Ring-billed Gull

Herring Gull
(first winter)

Caspian Tern

Forster's Tern
(fall)

Rock Dove

Yellow-billed Cuckoo

Eastern Screech-Owl
(gray phase)

Great Horned Owl

Barred Owl
(juvenile)

Northern Saw-whet Owl

Common Nighthawk

Belted Kingfisher
(female)

Red-headed Woodpecker

Downy Woodpecker

Northern Flicker

Willow Flycatcher

Eastern Phoebe

Eastern Kingbird

Horned Lark

Purple Martin
(juvenile)

Tree Swallow

Northern Rough-winged
Swallow

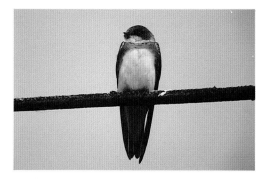

Bank Swallow

Barn Swallow

Carolina Chickadee

Tufted Titmouse

White-breasted Nuthatch

Brown Creeper

House Wren

Sedge Wren

Ruby-crowned Kinglet
(female)

Eastern Bluebird

American Robin
(female)

Northern Mockingbird

Brown Thrasher

Cedar Waxwing

Yellow-throated Vireo

Warbling Vireo

Red-eyed Vireo

Blue-winged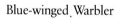 Warbler

Yellow Warbler

Yellow-rumped Warbler

Cerulean Warbler

American Redstart
(female)

Common Yellowthroat

Scarlet Tanager

Northern Cardinal

Indigo Bunting

Rufous-sided Towhee

Song Sparrow

White-crowned Sparrow

Bobolink

Red-winged Blackbird

Eastern Meadowlark

Common Grackle

Orchard Oriole

Northern Oriole

House Finch
(female)

Pine Siskin

American Goldfinch
(winter male)

Evening Grosbeak

House Sparrow

WOOD DUCK

Aix sponsa

Habitat: Backwaters of reservoirs, streams, canals, ponds, and lakes.
Local Sites: Backwaters of Eagle Creek, Geist, and Morse Reservoirs; Atterbury Fish and Wildlife Area; and most streams, rivers, and ponds. The Water Company canal in Broad Ripple is usually a good place to find them during the winter when they feed with other species of waterfowl.
Status: Common migrant and nesting species, usually arriving about the second week of March and remaining until early November. Some may remain during open-water winters.
Length: 18¹/₂ inches with a 28-inch wingspan.
Remarks: Touted by many as the most beautiful bird in North America, the drake Wood Duck certainly is eye-catching, sporting a multitude of bright hues in his glistening plumage. He courts a more subdued-looking female in early spring. Nesting takes place in April, with eggs being laid in a cavity such as an old woodpecker hole or a nesting box. The latter is often provided by the Department of Natural Resources or a bird-lover. They raise large broods, up to a dozen young in a clutch, as is common among waterfowl.

Long a favorite of hunters because of their fast, erratic flight and striking colors, Wood Ducks were at one time in serious jeopardy of becoming extinct. Thankfully, that danger is a thing of the past. They are probably one of the most photographed birds in the world: it's hard to pick up any wildlife calendar or set of greeting cards without seeing a resplendent drake Wood Duck somewhere in the pictures. They are also in demand as aviary specimens, being shipped to zoos and private collections throughout the world.

MALLARD

Anas platyrhynchos

Habitat: Backwaters of reservoirs, streams, canals, ponds, and lakes. The semi-domesticated variety can be found in urban and suburban drainage ditches and ponds, streams, and other habitat.

Local Sites: Atterbury Fish and Wildlife Area and the pond immediately behind the nature center at Eagle Creek Reservoir are good locations to see migrating Mallards. Semi-domesticated birds can be found just about anywhere.

Status: Abundant local resident. Like the Canada Goose, this species has become domesticated in central Indiana. The wild variety occurs from November through March, but such birds are sometimes difficult to separate from the domestic stock except for being more wary.

Length: 23 inches.

Remarks: Next to the chicken (Jungle Fowl) the Mallard is perhaps the most domesticated bird in the world, with various strains and hybrids populating our waterways, ponds, and lakes. The pure-strain Mallard drake, however, is one of our most beautiful ducks, with a satiny smooth greenish head coupled with a rusty breast and black and white body. While the domesticated version can be found breeding locally, the wild strain retreats to the prairie potholes of our northern states and southern Canada to breed. This species, like most other northern-breeding waterfowl, depends upon these prairie potholes to reproduce and maintain its population. In dry years when breeding has been curtailed or when a number of these areas have been drained, the fall migration tends to be reduced and hunting limits must be imposed to insure the species' survival. Fortunately, organizations like Ducks Unlimited and the Department of Fish and Wildlife spearhead the wise use of conservation through the establishment of breeding sanctuaries in the northern part of its range.

BLUE-WINGED TEAL

Anas discors

Habitat: Essentially the same as that of other waterfowl except that this species seems to prefer the smaller ponds or marshy lakes.

Local Sites: The shallow areas of reservoirs, particularly the north end of Eagle Creek Reservoir during migration and Atterbury Fish and Wildlife Area, where it has nested.

Status: Common migrant and rare nesting species. Appearing later in spring than most other waterfowl, usually the end of March until the second week in May, then reappearing in late July until the first to second week in October. Has bred locally at Atterbury Fish and Wildlife Area. Not known to winter.

Length: 15$^{1}/_{2}$ inches.

Remarks: Blue-wings when flying can usually be picked out from other waterfowl because of their much smaller size and the bright blue shoulder patches, and because they mimic the flight of shore-birds and some of the diving ducks as they gyrate back and forth over the marshy areas. They like to congregate in backwater sloughs with Northern Shovelers, Northern Pintails, Gadwalls, American Wigeons, and other puddle ducks. Fortunately Blue-wings remain a common migrant, no doubt because they can take advantage of an earlier fall flight when duck hunting is at a minimum and because they utilize a greater variety of shallow freshwater habitat. The female is brownish, but shares the large bluish patches on the forewing with the male bird.

CANVASBACK

Aythya valisineria

Habitat: Normally more of a deep water duck of the larger reservoirs and lakes.

Local Sites: All three reservoirs, Eagle Creek, Geist, and Morse. Sometimes gravel pits. Rarely found in shallow water habitat.

Status: Rare migrant and winter visitant, best seen in the months of March, November, and December; has been known to occur from November to early April. It breeds north of Indiana.

Length: 21 inches with a 34-inch wingspan.

Remarks: The male bird is strikingly patterned with a brick red head and neck, black chest, rump, vent, and tail, white sides and under-parts, and very pale gray to white back. Females are more drab in appearance, with a brown head, neck, and chest and a grayish body. Both sexes have a distinct profile; the head and bill are flattened and sloping to the extreme, somewhat like a caricature of Bob Hope. This species feeds by diving below the water to pick aquatic vegetation or to pursue invertebrates or small fish.

23

Canvasbacks will form large monotypic flocks when migrating but are more frequently seen in mixed flocks with scaup and Redheads.

Without a doubt this species is on the decline throughout Indiana and the Midwest. At one time they were fairly numerous, but now they are the least common, with the exception of the Greater Scaup, of the "bay ducks" to migrate through our area. Hunting pressure is only a minor contributor to this decline. Wetland losses in the bird's breeding range, the northwestern United States and southwestern Canada, and the use of lead shot are the major causes of the Canvasback's downward population trend. There are currently several joint ventures between the two governments to help alleviate this situation, so Canvasback numbers may show some improvements in the future.

LESSER SCAUP

Aythya affinis

Habitat: Large bodies of water, reservoirs, gravel/borrow pits.
Local Sites: All three nearby reservoirs, Eagle Creek, Geist, and Morse. Occasionally gravel/borrow pits.
Status: Common migrant, appearing about the end of March and remaining until mid-April; rarely later. In the fall the bulk of the migration occurs during November, with some birds remaining until freeze-up. Rarely winters.
Length: $16^1/_2$ inches.
Remarks: The Lesser Scaup is one of those ducks referred to as "bay ducks"—those that prefer the larger, deeper lakes. They also require a greater expanse of water surface to become airborne, partly because of feet positioned further back on their bodies. They fly in compact flocks that wheel to and fro over the feeding areas, making a pleasant picture of alternating black and white that recalls the aerial gyrations of a large flock of shorebirds.

Similar to the rarer Greater Scaup, this species reveals some slight anatomical differences. Once learned, they can help to separate it from that bird. Lessers have a distinctive head shape that usually shows a definite peak, while that of its larger relative is more rounded. There are other, more subtle, differences, like a reduced white wing stripe and a smaller nail area on the bill, that also help in identification.

HOODED MERGANSER

Lophodytes cucullatus

Habitat: Usually prefers the shallow areas of lakes, reservoirs, and ponds, where it consorts with the Wood Duck and nests like that species in holes in trees. Occasionally occurs in deeper water.

Local Sites: All three reservoirs, Eagle Creek, Geist, and Morse. Prefers the more heavily wooded streams and rivers in which to nest. A particularly good place to see them is behind the nature center at Eagle Creek Park in the waterfowl resting area.

Status: Fairly common migrant and very rare summer resident. The first migrants appear in March, and those that do not breed remain until late April. Fall birds can be found from late October until freeze-up. Then flocks of from four to as many as forty birds can be found, particularly in more sheltered places. Rarely winters. Breeding formerly took place at Eagle Creek Reservoir and in a marshy area in northern Marion County.

Length: 18 inches.

Remarks: The male Hooded Merganser is a splendid bird in its rich nuptial plumage of black, white, and chestnut which is sure to please even the most jaded birdwatcher. Early in the spring groups of displaying males will perform a courtship ritual of alternately expanding and contracting their handsome crests, hoping to entice the rather somber plumaged female that is the object of their ardor. In flight they can sometimes be recognized at a distance because of the rapid buzz-like quality of their wingbeats and the alternating black and white plumage of the male birds.

TURKEY VULTURE

Cathartes aura

Habitat: Can be seen soaring over open countryside and is occasionally seen high overhead even in more metropolitan areas.

Local Sites: Near the nature center at Eagle Creek Park a group of thirty to forty birds roost alongside the reservoir in tall dead trees.

Found frequently at Atterbury Fish and Wildlife Area and at Morgan-Monroe State Forest. The latter site can host considerable numbers.

Status: Common migrant and summer resident, appearing about the first to second week of March and remaining until late October, sometimes later. Has been reported during the winter in Morgan County.

Length: 27 inches. Wingspan 69 inches.

Remarks: Colloquially known as buzzards, Turkey Vultures are not true buzzards; that name is reserved for Europe's hawks of the genus Buteo. Vultures have an unsavory reputation because they are carrion eaters, something that is of great benefit in helping to clean up the environment. They are well adapted for their work: their heads are bare of feathers, and they possess the useful if rather disgusting habit of defecating on their feet. The highly acidic feces help kill any bacteria picked up from the carcasses on which they feed; this also has a cooling effect on the blood, which circulates in their legs and is then pumped through the rest of the body, cooling the entire bird in the process.

There is some dispute about whether vultures find food by sight or smell, both senses being highly developed. It is probably a combination of both. When frightened or agitated, they regurgitate and/or defecate to lighten the load, then take flight. Although believed by many to be incapable of sound, they can hiss vehemently when angered.

OSPREY

Pandion haliaetus

Habitat: Generally found soaring or perched near reservoirs and major streams and rivers.

Local Sites: All three reservoirs, Eagle Creek, Geist, and Morse plus White River. Rarely away from water except perhaps when migrating.

Status: Uncommon migrant, occurring mainly from March until mid-May and again from late July to October. Formerly nested in Morgan County. A definite increase in the population elsewhere in the Midwest may mean that the bird will resume breeding here.

Length: 22 inches with a 58-inch wingspan.

Remarks: The Osprey, or Fish Hawk as it is known colloquially, is the only North American raptor to exist wholly on a diet of fish. Their bodies are especially adapted for this purpose; they have long legs, razor-sharp talons, and small curved hooks on the soles of their feet for gripping slippery fish, which they take from the water while on the wing. On numerous occasions we have seen Ospreys stoop from heights to snatch goldfish, a favorite target, at great rates of speed.

They can be fussy eaters. One day in April while we were birding at Geist Reservoir, we spotted a bird actively hunting. It would swoop down and catch a Gizzard Shad, inspect what it had caught, and then drop it. This procedure was repeated seven times. Finally it came up clutching a Bluegill in its talons, alighted in a tree, and commenced to feed. Studies have shown, however, that the Osprey's diet is normally composed of rough fish.

BALD EAGLE

Haliaeetus leucocephalus

Habitat: Prefers larger lakes and reservoirs.

Local Sites: All three reservoirs, Eagle Creek, Geist, and Morse. Rarely found at Atterbury. Occasionally seen migrating very high along White River; rarely over the city.

Status: Rare migrant and winter visitant. Occurs most commonly during ice break-up when birds can feed upon the dead fish that usually come to the surface. Occasionally robs the Osprey of its catch. Recently found breeding in Morgan County. Birds are easily disturbed at their nest sites and these should be avoided if continued nesting is to occur.

Length: 32 inches with a wingspan of over 80 inches.

Remarks: Our national symbol, Bald Eagles are becoming a more familiar sight in the Midwest, and the potential for increased sightings in central Indiana is growing with the recent nesting of individuals on Lake Monroe and in Morgan County. Unfairly maligned in the past as livestock thieves, they feed primarily on fish and carrion and so are seldom very far from water.

Bald Eagles represent a triumph for conservation, for at one time they were very rarely seen. This was in large part due to the unrestricted use of pesticides such at DDT whose byproduct, DDE, caused excessive thinning of the birds' eggshells, which made them susceptible to breakage before the chicks could hatch. Thanks to the banning of many of these chemicals, the eagle has made a spectacular comeback. Currently the main danger to an eagle is the indiscriminate shooter who thinks any large bird is a good target.

During the late winter and into early spring these impressive birds begin their courtship rituals, soaring in twos and threes, locking talons and somersaulting through the air in a truly awe-inspiring display of aerial mastery. It's one of the things that everyone should have the opportunity to see at some point in their lifetime.

NORTHERN HARRIER

Circus cyaneus

Habitat: Likes to course over open fields seeking its prey, usually some unsuspecting mouse or vole.
Local Sites: Atterbury Fish and Wildlife Area: rarely occurs elsewhere.
Status: Formerly rather common, it is now a rare migrant and very rare nesting species. Can be found most frequently during the winter.
Length: Males, 18 inches; females up to 23 or 24 inches.
Remarks: Formerly known as the Marsh Hawk, the Northern Harrier is now unfortunately a rare sight in central Indiana. Changes in farming habits and/or a combination of pesticides have apparently impacted this species, like most of our larger birds of prey, negatively. It nested at Atterbury Fish and Wildlife Area as late as 1976, but no longer does so.

This species has a remarkable courtship flight that consists of "barrel rolls" with the bird, usually the male, turning sideways and rotating from side to side in a series of long, swooping dives. Like other hawks, this bird is what is termed "reversed sexually dimorphic," meaning that the females are larger than their male counterparts.

The Northern Harrier is one of those birds that deserves our protection, not only for the unquestioned good that it does in destroying rodents, but as a pleasing addition to our avifauna.

SHARP-SHINNED HAWK

Accipiter striatus

Habitat: Usually seen in dense woodlots and forests, where it strikes its prey with lightning speed. During migration can be found in a greater variety of habitat. Often seen migrating high overhead, sometimes in company with other hawks.

Local Sites: The heavily wooded areas of Eagle Creek Park, the Indianapolis Museum of Art grounds, Atterbury Fish and Wildlife Area, and Morgan-Monroe State Forest.

Status: Uncommon migrant and very rare nesting species. Occurs primarily during migration in April to early May and again in September and October. Rarely winters. Formerly nested but is not known to do so now.

Length: Male, 10 inches; female about 13–14 inches.

Remarks: We well recall the time we were banding Pine Siskins at the Indianapolis Museum of Art and an adult male sharpie careened into a mist net after an entrapped siskin. Had it not been for the fact that one of us was near the net when it happened, we might have missed its subsequent capture and banding.

This hawk could just as easily be called The Phantom of the Woods, appearing and disappearing with a rapidity that would dazzle most birds if not the human observer. They seem to be in high gear all the time as they dash among the trees in pursuit of their prey, alternately gliding and flapping and using their rather long tails to maneuver through the dense canopy of the forest.

Although they do not endear themselves to people who dislike hawks' "heartless pursuit of sweet little songbirds," they nevertheless perform a useful function in eliminating weaker birds that are less adept at escape.

COOPER'S HAWK

Accipiter cooperii

Habitat: Dense woodlots and forests. During migration, found in a more varied habitat. Preys mostly on larger birds, such as pigeons, doves, and robins.

Local Sites: Found in the same areas as the Sharp-shinned Hawk: Eagle Creek Park, Atterbury Fish and Wildlife Area, Indianapolis Museum of Art grounds. During the winter, often seen at bird feeders in urban and suburban locations.

Status: Fairly common migrant and uncommon nesting species. Nests have been found at Eagle Creek Park, Atterbury Fish and Wildlife Area, Morgan-Monroe State Forest, and Riverside Park. Probably nests elsewhere. Migrants appear in April and, during the fall, in October. Some winter in favored localities.

Length: Males 14 inches, females up to 20 inches.

Remarks: Traditionally known to farmers as the Chicken Hawk, Cooper's Hawks very seldom prey on anything as large as a chicken. Up to 85 percent of the diet of this species is composed of birds ranging in size from sparrows to pigeons.

Accipiters, the Latin generic name for this family of hawks, have relatively short wings in proportion to body length. This helps them maneuver through heavy brush and foliage. For the same reason, their tails are disproportionately long to serve as rudders. Very fast, strong fliers, they are the scourge of bird feeders, which they see as easy hunting grounds. This habit of raiding bird feeders is one reason for the Cooper's Hawk's bad reputation and has been the cause of more than one collision with a picture window in the course of high-speed pursuit. They also exhibit the curious behavior of chasing wounded prey on the ground. With their long legs they look rather ungainly, running and hopping and resembling nothing so much as an arrogant, undersized turkey.

This species is an active defender of its nest site and will attack any intruder with vigor. The nest is generally placed twenty to thirty feet up in a coniferous tree that is heavily foliaged. From two to four young are raised each nesting season and require constant care and feeding.

RED-SHOULDERED HAWK

Buteo lineatus

Habitat: Prefers heavily forested areas, but will hunt over open fields.
Local Sites: Eagle Creek Park and Morgan-Monroe State Forest. Occasionally seen at Atterbury Fish and Wildlife Area.
Status: Rare migrant and nesting species. Forty years ago this was the common Buteo in the Indianapolis area. Today, for whatever reason, the bird has become quite rare and is officially listed as a species of special concern by the Nongame Program of the Indiana DNR Division of Fish and Wildlife. Part of this rarity could be the result of competition from the now more abundant Red-tailed Hawk, which seems to have filled the niche once occupied by this species.
Length: Averages about 19 inches, with a wingspan up to 40 inches.
Remarks: Red-shouldered Hawks are extremely beneficial birds, taking a large proportion of harmful rodents and insects. Bent relates that of 220 stomachs examined by the Biological Survey, 102 contained mice; 92, insects; 40, other mammals; 39, frogs; 20, reptiles; 16, spiders; 12, other birds; 7, crawfish; 3, poultry; 3, fish; 2, offal; and 1, earthworms. The fact that the bird deserves protection can therefore be little disputed.

Although it is a rare breeder, we found a nest of this species in 1976 near the nature center at Eagle Creek Park. It was located about forty feet up in a Norway Spruce. We banded three chicks. One of us still bears the scars of that encounter: one of the young birds decided that it was not too crazy about being handled.

RED-TAILED HAWK

Buteo jamaicensis

Habitat: Found nearly everywhere. Can be seen soaring over open fields as well as forests. Most often seen, however, as they sit along roadways on fence posts, telephone poles, or in trees, on the watch for the small rodents that make up the bulk of their diet.

Local Sites: Nests at Atterbury Fish and Wildlife Area, Morgan-Monroe State Forest, Eagle Creek Park, and several other areas.

Status: Common migrant, fairly common nesting species and winter resident. Migrants from farther north begin to move into the Indianapolis area in October and November, and peak numbers for this species usually occur at this time.

Length: 22 inches, with a wingspan of approximately 51 inches.

Remarks: Year-round residents, Red-tails begin nesting in March and April, building a nest out of sticks placed high up in the canopy of a tree. From two to four white eggs are laid, and hatching occurs in May. The fledglings are usually out of the nest by the end of June but remain in the vicinity until the end of summer.

Although they are often harassed by smaller birds their only real threat comes from people and from the highly competitive Great Horned Owl. These owls have been known to kill Red-tails so that they can take over prime nesting sites.

AMERICAN KESTREL

Falco sparverius

Habitat: Often seen sitting on telephone lines or hovering alongside roads where they prey almost exclusively on small insects and rodents. Kestrels also visit feeders during the winter where they capture small birds.

Local Sites: Found in open fields and suburban areas of the Indianapolis region. Atterbury Fish and Wildlife Area with its open fields is a good place to see this bird year round. Will nest in Wood Duck or Screech Owl boxes, and in old woodpecker holes. A pair even nests on the grounds of the Indianapolis Zoo.

Status: Fairly common migrant and nesting species. Common during the winter.

Length: 10$^1/_2$ inches.

Remarks: Previously called the Sparrow Hawk, the colorful American Kestrel is our smallest hawk. It is beneficial to mankind, as it feeds primarily on a variety of small insects and rodents. The kestrel first captures its prey in its razor-sharp talons, then sharply twists its neck with its bill, thus administering the *coup de grâce*. The kestrel's bill is well designed for this method of killing because of a notch about halfway back that provides additional leverage and holding ability.

American Kestrels are avid hunters, highly persistent in the pursuit of prey. During banding operations, we have seen them repeatedly attack bait in traps before becoming ensnared. Occasionally they take large birds; one female killed several Mourning Doves daily, eating only the brains and leaving the rest. Members of the falcon family, kestrels are fast fliers, easily overtaking even the speediest quarry.

PEREGRINE FALCON

Falco peregrinus

Habitat: Found in a wide variety of habitat, both urban and suburban. Migrates over open country as well as along river courses.

Local Sites: In 1991 the Indiana DNR Division of Fish and Wildlife Nongame Program released fifteen young birds (this is called hacking) in downtown Indianapolis, where the large buildings mimic the species' traditional clifftop nesting sites and pigeons are a convenient source of food. During the spring of 1992 one of these birds paired up with another in metropolitan Cincinnati. At the time of this writing, twelve of the birds were successfully fledged; it is hoped that when they return from migrating at least one pair will eventually use this area to nest. Prior to the 1991 hacking attempt, a pair of birds released earlier at a Minnesota site took up residence in downtown Indianapolis, but did not breed. Eagle Creek Reservoir is a good area to spot migrating birds.

Status: Rare migrant, becoming more common in recent years due to restocking at various sites in the Midwest. Very rare during the winter.

Length: Males $15^{1}/_{2}$ inches, females up to $19^{1}/_{2}$ inches.

Remarks: It is doubtful that the Peregrine Falcon was ever a common nesting species in central Indiana, even in the days of the early settlers, because there were no suitable nesting sites. This species is largely a cliff dweller, utilizing high, rocky outcrops like those found in the Appalachians and the Rocky Mountains as well as other areas in the West. It probably did occur during migration, but apparently was a rare bird even then.

After World War II, conservationists, ornithologists, and bird-watchers noted an alarming decline in this species in that part of its range where it was a familiar nesting bird; investigators at nest sites found that the birds were laying extremely thin-shelled eggs that broke under the adult birds' weight during incubation. Chemical analysis revealed that the cause of this eggshell thinning was the by-product DDE of the pesticide DDT, which was stored up in the birds' fatty tissue. This harmful chemical was banned in the United States in 1972.

Then, largely through the efforts of some dedicated scientists, a peregrine hatching program was initiated using eggs from healthy adult birds. Young were then restocked (hacked) in strategic areas. Will the peregrine population be able to rebound? Fortunately, the answer appears to be yes.

The adult peregrine is a model of flight perfection, reaching air speeds of over 200 mph in pursuit of its prey. Those lucky enough to have witnessed these flights marvel at the birds' uncanny aerial gyrations.

WILD TURKEY

Meleagris gallopavo

Habitat: Forests bordering cornfields, in which they usually feed.
Local Sites: At present confined to Atterbury Fish and Wildlife Area and Morgan-Monroe State Forest.
Status: Very rare permanent resident. Restocked at the above locations. Most likely to be seen during the early morning when they feed at bordering fields or when the males are strutting, gobbling, and courting in early April.
Length: Males nearly 48 inches, females 36 inches.
Remarks: Benjamin Franklin regretted that the Wild Turkey had not been chosen as our national bird. The eagle, he wrote, was "a bird of bad moral character," lazy, and "a rank coward," whereas the turkey is "a much more respectable bird" and, "though a little vain and silly,

. . . a bird of courage." At one point Wild Turkeys were extirpated from the state because of overhunting, but, thanks to restocking efforts by the Indiana Department of Natural Resources and strict hunting regulations, they are once again reasonably common in certain areas. A short hunting season is allowed each spring so that hunters can have an opportunity to test their skills against this wily bird. Most return empty-handed due to the wary nature of the turkey.

Turkeys eat a wide assortment of berries, nuts, and insects and are most frequently spotted either feeding or running swiftly from danger. They form large roosts in winter—up to fifty birds—frequenting pine groves at night and feeding in the fields and woods by day. Progenitors of the domestic turkey, Wild Turkeys nest on the ground and like most gallinaceous birds lay large clutches of eggs, up to thirteen per nest. Nests are very well camouflaged and difficult to locate.

Turkey feathers have long been used by humans for a variety of purposes: by the American Indians for arrow fletching; by early settlers for quill pens; and by fishermen for fly-tying. Turkey eggs and of course the turkey itself provide sustenance for people yet today.

SORA

Porzana carolina

Habitat: Marshes, fens, and the low, cattailed periphery of ponds and lakes. With their extremely long toes they can move about easily on floating vegetation without sinking in.

Local Sites: The north marshy end of Eagle Creek and Geist Reservoirs and the ice-skating ponds at Eagle Creek Park. Also at Atterbury Fish and Wildlife Area, particularly Furnace Fen.

Status: Fairly common migrant. Formerly bred and may still do so, but no recent nesting records. Occurs primarily in April and early May and again in September and October.

Length: 8¹/₂ inches.

Remarks: The Sora has the characteristic plump profile of the rail family; but, unlike the Virginia Rail, the other species of rail that one is likely to see, it has a short, yellow, cootlike bill. Adults are mostly brown backed, have a gray face and breast, and sport a black bib, yellow legs, and black and white vertical striping on their flanks. Young birds are buffier than adults and lack the adults' black bib.

The nest, a small floating platform made of aquatic vegetation, supports up to a dozen small eggs. Downy young are precocious and are coal black in color with a whitish beak and legs. Soras will call all year long, a loud descending whinny or a loud two-syllable "ker-weee," but are most vocal in May and June. They feed on small aquatic insects, worms, crustaceans, and fish, which they pick out of the floating vegetation along the water's edge. When startled or pressured they swim quite buoyantly from cover to cover in an attempt to escape. Soras are very weak fliers and seldom go more than one hundred feet at a time unless engaged in long-distance migration.

AMERICAN COOT

Fulica americana

Habitat: May be found virtually anywhere, especially bordering marshy areas, where there is sufficient water expanse to enable the bird to become airborne.

Local Sites: All three reservoirs, Eagle Creek, Geist, and Morse, during migration. Probably has nested at Atterbury Fish and Wildlife Area. Some birds have been seen at Eagle Creek Reservoir during June and July, which suggests nesting.

Status: Common migrant, appearing from late March until the first week of May. Returning birds can be seen between late September and late November. Sometimes will remain during mild winters. These midwinter populations are low due to a lack of available open water, but on lakes that remain ice-free large concentrations can accumulate in a relatively small area.

Length: 15$^1/_2$ inches with a wingspan of 25 inches.

Remarks: Despite its superficial resemblance to a duck, the American Coot is actually a member of the rail family. Its bill is conical and compressed laterally rather than flattened like a duck's and its toes are lobed instead of webbed. The dark, slate-gray plumage of a coot is distinctive, as are its white bill and the pumping motion it displays while swimming. With their plump bodies and short wings coots are weak fliers at best. They prefer to swim away from danger, and when induced to fly they require considerable takeoff distances to become airborne. Once aloft, they expend a great deal of energy sustaining flight, flapping rapidly with no soaring, and land with all the grace of a thrown rock.

Coots associate freely with ducks of all species as well as grebes, and are usually seen in either monotypic or mixed flocks rather than singly. They feed on aquatic vegetation and invertebrates and are often found grazing on the mown grass of golf courses, cemeteries, and city parks. Nesting in dense cattails, they construct an anchored platform, composed of dead stalks of that plant and other vegetation, that can range in size from one to two feet in diameter. Up to a dozen eggs are laid; these are ovate in shape and are a rich tan color heavily blotched with dark brown. Downy chicks are heavily colored with rusty red about the head, breast, shoulders, and throat and have a bicolored red and black bill. Immatures resemble the adults but are a much lighter gray on the throat and breast.

SANDHILL CRANE

Grus canadensis

Habitat: Found in this area in cornfields while migrating or rarely in marshy habitat.

Local Sites: Migrant birds can be noted high overhead during migration or during brief stopovers in areas where feeding is good. Can frequently be seen at Atterbury Fish and Wildlife Area and Eagle Creek Reservoir.

Status: Uncommon to common migrant, appearing from late February until the first of April and returning in November and early December. There is at least one record of a wintering bird at Atterbury Fish and Wildlife Area.

Length: About 42 inches with a wingspan over six feet.

Remarks: The great ornithologist Elliott Coues was aptly quoted in Bent in regard to migrating sandhills: "Such ponderous bodies, moving with slowly-beating wings, give a great idea of momentum from mere weight—of force in motion without swiftness; for they plod along heavily, seeming to need every inch of their ample wings to sustain themselves. One would think they must soon alight fatigued with such exertion, but the raucous cries continue, and the birds fly on for miles along the tortuous stream, in Indian file, under some trusty leader, who croaks his hoarse orders, implicitly obeyed."

One of the true conservation success stories of our age is the continued increase of this species throughout the Midwest, particularly in our area. Forty years ago it was a red-letter day when birders could say that they had seen some of these birds in central Indiana. Now such observations are rather commonplace. Local area birders who wish to see the bird in maximum abundance, however, annually make the 120-mile trip north to Jasper-Pulaski Fish and Wildlife Area in northern Indiana. Here, during the fall, impressive numbers of these birds can be noted at dusk, coming into the refuge to roost. The Department of Natural Resources estimate of the maximum fall assemblage during mid-November 1991 was 32,000 birds, an all-time high count that may have been precipitated by the dry summer in the Midwest, which tended to concentrate the birds into this one area.

KILLDEER

Charadrius vociferus

Habitat: Nests in the gravel areas of dirt roads, parking lots, exposed gravel bars of creeks and rivers. Feeds in a wide variety of habitat from golf courses to cemeteries and open lawns. Congregates during the fall on the periphery of lakes and reservoirs.
Local Sites: Easily found in the above habitat in this area; congregates at Eagle Creek, Geist, and Morse Reservoirs in the fall.
Status: Common migrant and summer resident. In the spring the first birds arrive during the late February warm-up and remain until the middle of December. They occasionally winter during warm years.
Length: $10^{1}/_{2}$ inches.
Remarks: The Latin nomenclature for this species is certainly most appropriate—it means noisy plover. Old-time gunners considered it a pest on hunting grounds because it spooked so easily, giving its pene-

trating "kill-deer" or "kill-dee" calls, thus flushing other more desirable birds.

The nest is simply a hollowed-out scrape in the gravel and can be located on flat rooftops, driveways, or sandbars. Its habit of using driveways puts it in close proximity to humans, so it is a familiar bird to many. Killdeers exhibit behavior known as injury feigning when disturbed at their nests. The female will attempt to lead the potential predator or interloper, whether human or otherwise, away from the nest by crying piteously and pretending to have a broken wing. In most cases this is effective, and when the danger has passed the bird will return to the nest. The four eggs are neatly arranged with the small ends pointed inward and can be deceptively hard to see against the background of gravel or loose stones. Baby Killdeers are miniature editions of the adult, sporting the same color configuration. They are what is termed precocial, or able to move about soon after hatching, and nearly independent of the parents for food or care. Occasionally, however, during wet springs we have seen young birds get mud balls around the bottom of their feet. If these are allowed to dry the bird is unable to feed itself and soon expires.

LESSER YELLOWLEGS

Tringa flavipes

Habitat: Shallow marshy areas, wet fields ("skyponds"), and the partially dried periphery of ponds and lakes.
Local Sites: All three reservoirs, Eagle Creek, Geist, and Morse. Can be found quite frequently at Atterbury Fish and Wildlife Area.
Status: Common migrant, appearing in early April through the second week of May. Reappearing as early as July until mid-October, rarely into November.
Length: 10$^1/_2$ inches.
Remarks: Those of us who love shorebirds look forward each spring and fall to the return of the Lesser Yellowlegs. They are the spirit of the shallow water bogs, marshes, rain-filled fields, and mudflats of our reservoirs. Here they feed, sometimes in a mixed flock of other shorebirds along with their larger cousin, the Greater Yellowlegs, which

they closely resemble except for differences in voice, size, and bill configuration. They share with some other shorebirds the habit of tilting forward and backward as they rest between feeding forays. The reason is not known, but the custom seems to be found in a wide variety of species that inhabit waterways, including some songbirds.

A noisy bird like the Killdeer, when flushed it emits a rather loud, far-carrying, "tew-tew-tew-tew," sometimes given in singles, couplets, or more depending on whether or not the bird was disturbed. When this happens it usually circles the area and quite often lands nearby where it again resumes feeding.

SPOTTED SANDPIPER

Actitis macularia

Habitat: Sandbars of creeks and rivers. The dried periphery of lakes, ponds, and reservoirs. In general, prefers a more rocky substrate.
Local Sites: All three reservoirs, Eagle Creek, Geist, and Morse. Nests on sandbars of White River and the border of some gravel or borrow pits.
Status: Common migrant and nesting species. Arrives in early April and departs about mid-October.
Length: $7^1/_2$ inches.
Remarks: Spotted Sandpipers have a striking spring plumage in which both sexes show spotted underparts. These spots are absent later in the year after they have completed their late summer molt. They are easy to distinguish at any time of the year by their low flight over the water with rapidly moving, stiff wingbeats, somewhat reminiscent of a moth, a type of motion that is unusual in shorebirds. This characteristic is coupled with a loud, penetrating call of "pereet-reet-reet" as they flush before an observer walking along the side of some stream of lake. Like several other shorebirds it has the peculiar and little understood habit of teetering, with the entire body moving forward and backward while the legs and feet remain stationary. This species is also more prone to perching on snags than any other water-oriented member of the shorebird family in our area.

The nest, a mere grass-lined depression in the ground, is usually located in rather open areas of dry fields and pastures normally along the edges of lakes or streams. The usual clutch is four eggs. We found one pair nesting in the middle of an old cinder road at the Indianapolis Sewage Disposal Plant near one of the former filtration ponds that were characteristic of that area years ago. When flushed from the nest the parent bird gave a distraction display feigning a broken wing, similar to the display of the Killdeer. Upon hatching, young birds spring into almost immediate action and run along the ground, teetering much like their parents.

UPLAND SANDPIPER

Bartramia longicauda

Habitat: Old fields, airports, and sod farms.
Local Sites: Formerly at Atterbury Fish and Wildlife Area, Stout Field, and Allison Plant No. 5. Now restricted to Indianapolis International Airport.
Status: Very rare summer resident and migrant. Spring birds arrive about mid-April and remain in breeding areas until about the first week of September.
Length: 12 inches.
Remarks: The Upland Sandpiper or Upland Plover, as it used to be called, is now relegated to endangered status by the Indiana DNR Division of Fish and Wildlife Nongame Program. It is an atypical shorebird in that it has restricted itself to the open prairie or grassland areas of the state where it was formerly more abundant. Shrinkage of available habitat through changes in farming practices and real estate encroachment has sadly reduced the present population.

This species has an unusual courtship flight in which the birds fly up into the sky until they are mere specks and then give a clear, tremulous whistle that is quite pleasing to the ear. They then fold their wings and drop toward the ground, adroitly landing with wings raised up over their backs. At other times their flight closely resembles that of the smaller Spotted Sandpiper, with stiff, shallow, rapid wingbeats, but otherwise the two species are quite different. Both sexes also like to perch on fence posts or even telephone wires.

The nest is usually well hidden in thick grass and consists of a slight hollow lined with pieces of dry grass. Here the female lays her four pinkish eggs which she incubates for about twenty-one days. Upon hatching, the young birds are extremely difficult to discern, and when closely approached the female bird will try to draw the observer or predator away by behaving as though wounded, flopping about with beak open as if panting, all the while emitting a pitiful cry. The young birds are precocious and are able to feed by themselves within hours of hatching.

Although some habitat is still available at airports, the species needs large tracts of nondisturbed grassy areas.

SEMIPALMATED SANDPIPER

Calidris pusilla

Habitat: The periphery of partially dried lakes, reservoirs, and fish hatcheries.
Local Sites: All three reservoirs during dry years—Eagle Creek, Geist, and Morse. Occasionally found frequenting rain-filled fields.
Status: Common migrant in appropriate habitat, appearing about mid-May until the first week of June. Fall birds begin migrating soon after young are hatched, appearing in July with late birds remaining until October.
Length: 6¼ inches.
Remarks: This bird's common name derives from the partial webbing located at the base of its toes. One of a group of small sandpipers collectively known as peeps, the Semipalmated is a diminutive bird, exceptionally small for a member of the shorebird family. All of the peeps are very similar in appearance but this species has the shortest bill, which has a somewhat bulbous tip, and black legs. They often associate with Least Sandpipers, gleaning insects and worms from the mudflats, beaches, and riprap surrounding the lakes and ponds of central Indiana. Flocks in flight do some spectacular formation flying. They fly at high speed, zigzagging with remarkable synchronization without missing a wingbeat.

This species is a long distance migrant, breeding in arctic Canada and Alaska but spending the winters in Central and South America. Their choice of winter grounds is somewhat hazardous for them as they comprise a major source of protein in the local diet in many South American countries. Peregrine Falcons are the Semipalmated's other main predator, but they take relatively few in comparison to the losses generated by human activities.

PECTORAL SANDPIPER

Calidris melanotos

Habitat: The periphery of partially dried lakes, reservoirs, and fish hatcheries. Occasionally found in heavier vegetation and grass.
Local Sites: All three reservoirs, Eagle Creek, Geist, and Morse, Atterbury Fish and Wildlife Area, and skyponds.
Status: Common migrant from mid-March until the first week in May, then again in early July until late October and rarely into November.
Length: 8³/₄ inches.
Remarks: The heavy rains that usually occur in late March and early April produce what birders call skyponds in the lower parts of farm fields and surrounding areas. This type of habitat is often frequented by yellowlegs. Around the periphery, where the grass or emergent crops are beginning to develop, a group of brownish shorebirds with clearly differentiated chest markings may be found. These are the Pectoral Sandpipers, back from their winter quarters, on their way to the Arctic tundra to breed. They are smaller than the nearby yellowlegs and somewhat squatty in appearance. If a predator happens to appear they flush *en masse* in a dense flock and begin to gyrate through the sky in a series of avoidance procedures that would put any jet pilot to shame. Veering from side to side, they first show their brownish backs and then their whiter underparts, resembling, to our eyes, a handful of confetti thrown into the wind. As soon as the predator departs the whole flock usually returns to the same or a nearby area to recommence their feeding.

Pectoral Sandpipers typify what non-birders think of when they hear the word sandpiper—smallish, brown, nondescript birds of the shoreline that feed by probing in the mud and travel in large flocks.

They get their name partly from the rather sharp, clear-cut brownish chest markings that form a distinct bib and also from the fact that on their breeding grounds the male bird enlarges his breast area in a courtship ritual. This ritual is curiously similar to that of courting prairie-chickens during which a group of males try to attract the attention of a nearby female, all the while emitting a low hooting call which is uttered frequently.

COMMON SNIPE

Gallinago gallinago

Habitat: Low swampy or marshy areas, drainage ditches, and skyponds.

Local Sites: Can be found anywhere there are low wet areas, but perhaps the best spot is Atterbury Fish and Wildlife Area in the fall of the year.

Status: Common migrant. Spring birds usually appear in mid-March and the migration continues until about the first week of May. In the fall the bulk of the migrants go through in September and October with some tarrying until December. Occasionally winters in low wet areas free of ice.

Length: $10^1/_2$ inches.

Remarks: Virtually everyone has heard of going on a snipe hunt, but very few people realize that there really is such a creature as a snipe. A rotund, long-billed member of the shorebird family, the Common Snipe is a denizen of open wet or boggy areas in central Indiana during its migration. Well camouflaged, they are most often seen when they explode from cover underfoot and take to rapid and erratic flight, uttering a short, loud alarm call.

Although it is not normally seen or heard in central Indiana, the spring courtship flight consists of the males flying to great heights and rapidly swooping groundward toward a female. The speed produced by dropping creates a fluttering sound, called winnowing, that apparently emanates from the stiff outer tail feathers, which can be heard for quite some distance.

Snipe spend a great deal of time feeding, probing into the mud with their long flexible bills in search of worms, leeches, and other invertebrates. Their muted, intricate patterns of browns, tans, and buffs make them difficult to distinguish from their surroundings. It takes a sharp eye to pick out a snipe in cover. They sometimes associate with other species of shorebirds but as a rule they are generally found further back from the water than most sandpipers.

Snipe are considered gamebirds and are hunted in most states, although the sport is more popular in the South than it is locally; here, most sportsmen prefer a shotgun to the legendary burlap bag and flashlight.

AMERICAN WOODCOCK

Scolopax minor

Habitat: Low wet or boggy spots in forested areas.
Local Sites: Eagle Creek Park, Atterbury Fish and Wildlife Area, and other local areas where there is sufficient habitat.
Status: Fairly common migrant and summer resident, but seldom seen because of its cryptic coloration and secretive habits. Arriving birds can be found about the first of March with departure in October and November.
Length: 11 inches.
Remarks: The so-called Timber Doodle is an inhabitant of the wet boggy woodlands. In March we have witnessed the courtship flight of male birds at dusk at Eagle Creek Park as they mount up in the sky, giving a twittering call, then descend to the ground where they strut their stuff before an onlooking female bird. Although they probably set up housekeeping there, we have never been fortunate enough to find the nest, probably because it is so well camouflaged and the young blend in so well with their surroundings.

Woodcocks, gamebirds like the Common Snipe, have long, flexible bills with which they probe the wet soil in search of earthworms or other sustenance. Interestingly, we know of occasions where birds have frequented wet lawns, particularly after a heavy rain, in search of their favorite prey. In addition to the long bill they also have large eyes that enable them to see particularly well at dusk or in the darkness of the woods that they frequently inhabit. They can occasionally be seen late in the day, just at nightfall, as they move from one feeding area to another. Because they normally fly low to the ground they are frequently vulnerable to being hit by automobiles and are sometimes noted as road casualties.

Next time you are out in the wet woods in late March be sure to make the acquaintance of this most interesting bird.

BONAPARTE'S GULL

Larus philadelphia

Habitat: Lakes, reservoirs, gravel pits, and river valleys during migration.
Local Sites: All three nearby reservoirs, Eagle Creek, Geist, and Morse. Sometimes seen migrating along White River and at local area gravel pits.
Status: Uncommon migrant, appearing in late March up to mid-April during the spring. The southbound migration occurs in late October and stretches into early December.
Length: $13^1/_2$ inches with a wingspan of 33 inches.
Remarks: This small gull is among the most beautiful and dainty of the Larids (gull genus). Breeding plumaged adults have a black head, with white crescents above and below the eye, a black bill, and black trailing edges to the primaries and secondaries. Underparts, tail, nape, and the outer four to five primaries and their coverts are a brilliant white, offsetting the gray mantle and bright red legs. In winter plumage they lose the black head, retaining only a round black spot behind the eye. Young birds have more black in the primaries, a brownish carpal bar, brownish secondaries, and a thin black subterminal band on the tail.

The flight of the Bonaparte's Gull is much more buoyant than that of the larger gulls. They have the ability to hover for short periods and frequently patter about over the surface of the water as they pick up small fish and insects. Bonies (as they are often called) will dive into the water from low heights in pursuit of their dinners and are willing to walk the shoreline gleaning bits of food from the mud and sand.

They are not above resorting to piracy in order to get a meal, and they frequently rob scaup, mergansers, and goldeneye when they surface with food. In turn, the Bonaparte's themselves are harassed by larger gulls and jaegers, being forced to drop or disgorge fish in order to get away from their persecutors. Unlike Ring-billed Gulls, Bonies are seldom seen very far from large bodies of water.

RING-BILLED GULL

Larus delawarensis

Habitat: Large reservoirs, lakes, and river valleys.
Local Sites: Eagle Creek, Geist, and Morse Reservoirs. They can frequently be seen on White River in the vicinity of the rapids just below the Kentucky Avenue bridge.
Status: Common migrant and winter visitant. Occurs from September though May. Can occasionally be seen during the summer when young birds or non-breeding adults often occur. Nests in northwest Indiana.
Length: $17^1/_2$ inches with a wingspan of nearly 48 inches.
Remarks: The Ring-billed Gull is the commonest of the "seagulls" encountered in central Indiana and can even be spotted well away from water during migration. Large flocks are often seen roosting and feeding on golf courses, baseball diamonds, and farm fields. Normally, however, they are associated with lakes and rivers where they feed on fish, insects, and a large variety of refuse products. Gulls are one of the few species of birds that have actually benefited from human activities; landfills serve as major feeding areas during the winter. As is the case with all gulls, Ring-bills undergo a multitude of plumage changes and can be difficult to identify for the neophyte. Fortunately they are quite tame and can be lured in for close-up looks with popcorn or bread. Because of their tameness one of the better locations to study them is in areas where domestic ducks are kept and fed. In the spring, when farmers are plowing their fields, large flocks of these birds will congregate behind the tractors and feast on disturbed in-

sects. As with Herring Gulls, Ring-bills pirate food from feeding mergansers, primarily the Red-breasted.

All gulls are exquisite fliers; they can soar for long periods and are capable of high-speed maneuvers in gale force winds. Highly gregarious, they are most often seen migrating in flocks, seldom as single birds.

HERRING GULL

Larus argentatus

Habitat: Prefers the larger reservoirs and rivers.
Local Sites: Eagle Creek, Geist, and Morse Reservoirs and White River valley.
Status: Uncommon migrant and winter visitant from late November until the first of April. Most often seen in colder weather.
Length: 25 inches with a wingspan of 58 inches.
Remarks: Larger than the Ring-billed Gull by about one-third, Herring Gulls are not as common and are seldom seen very far from large bodies of water. They attain adult plumage at the end of a four-year cycle as opposed to the three-year cycle displayed by the Ring-bills but can look similar to an inexperienced observer. Varying considerably in color during the maturation process, from dark brown to white and gray, they can be mistaken for different species when in reality they are only different ages. There is nearly as much variation in color among age groups as there is in size among subspecies.

Herring Gulls are aggressive feeders and will attempt to eat anything. They have been seen carrying and attempting to swallow fishing lures, six-pack liners, fishing line, and pieces of tin cans, and this voraciousness has proved deadly on more than one occasion. Their habit of scavenging is useful to humans, however, as it helps keep beaches and harbors free from dead fish and refuse.

As with other gulls, mergansers of all three species are subject to piracy by Herring Gulls. The gulls follow feeding flocks of mergansers, waiting for one to capture a fish, at which point the gulls mob the unfortunate victim and steal his dinner. Egg stealing by this species has become a major problem in tern colonies on the East Coast.

This habit has always been there, but population increases by the gulls are seriously aggravating the situation. In many locations programs are underway to control population levels among the gulls, thereby reducing tern predation.

Herring Gulls follow the ice line south as winter progresses, staying just one step ahead of total freeze-up. Hardy birds, they seem little affected by the cold; we have seen numbers of them standing on the ice when the wind chill temperature was nearly seventy degrees below zero.

CASPIAN TERN

Sterna caspia

Habitat: Reservoirs, lakes, and to a lesser extent river valleys. Nests farther north in Michigan and Wisconsin.

Local Sites: Eagle Creek, Geist, and Morse Reservoirs. Occasionally gravel pits and White River.

Status: Uncommon migrant, appearing about mid-April to the first of May. The southbound migration occurs during September and continues until the first of October.

Length: 21 inches with a wingspan of 50 inches.

Remarks: This is the largest of the North American terns and is more likely to be confused with a gull than with another species of tern. Owing, at least in part, to their great size, they are more aggressive than other terns and will rob the smaller species of their prey and, when available, will steal and eat the eggs and young. The majority of a Caspian Tern's diet is comprised of small fish, mostly minnows and baby shad, taken by skimming close to the water's surface and picking them up or by diving into the water head first and grabbing them. As with other terns, this species' call is harsh and unmelodic. It consists of a loud, abrasive "skraaa" that can be heard for quite some distance and is unlike the call of the gulls and other, lesser terns.

During the spring, summer, and fall they locate for the most part around freshwater impoundments, but in winter months they are less selective and will spend time on the seacoasts. Caspian Terns do more resting on the water than any of the other species of terns in Indiana although they are more regularly seen standing in the company of gulls on sandy or rocky shorelines and islands.

FORSTER'S TERN

Sterna forsteri

Habitat: Reservoirs, lakes, and river valleys.
Local Sites: Eagle Creek, Geist, and Morse Reservoirs. Frequents gravel and borrow pits and White River.
Status: Uncommon migrant appearing in April through May and again reappearing in late August until about mid-October.
Length: $14^{1}/_{2}$ inches with a wingspan of 31 inches.
Remarks: This attractive, graceful, delicate bird is only a migrant through the Indianapolis area. Similar to the Common Tern (which is not common here), the Forster's Tern lacks the dark outer primaries of that species and, in winter plumage, has a black auricular (ear) patch as opposed to the dark crown of the Common. All terns' legs are exceptionally short for a bird of their size so that they waddle ungracefully when walking, but once in the air they are masters of flight, highly maneuverable and quick.

Terns in the genus *Sterna* feed on small fish and insects and are harassed routinely by larger gulls into dropping their dinner in acts of aerial piracy. The upsurge in large gull populations has had a detrimental effect on tern populations, because the gulls also raid tern nests and devour their eggs and young; however, it is loss of nesting habitat that is the major contributor to declines in Forster's Tern numbers. To reproduce they require freshwater marshes, one of the most rapidly declining habitats in North America.

ROCK DOVE

Columba livia

Habitat: The Rock Dove or pigeon is found virtually everywhere there is human activity of some kind, but in particular on bridge overpasses, steel tresses, and buildings, where they nest. It has been said that the building of the interstate system has been responsible for the species' widespread increase. Large flocks are often seen in the vicinity of grain elevators and farm lots.

Local Sites: Metropolitan Indianapolis and surrounding grain elevator lots.

Status: Common permanent resident.

Length: 12$\frac{1}{2}$ inches.

Remarks: All too often, we tend to take for granted those things which are commonly found about us. A classic example is the ubiquitous pigeon or Rock Dove. Originally a native of the continent of Europe, where it still breeds fairly commonly in such localities as the white cliffs of Dover, the pigeon was transported physically by some of our forefathers to the new world. Here it has become, to many of us, an unwelcome pest. Its habits create unsanitary conditions and often lead indirectly to such airborne diseases as histoplasmosis. Then, too, their unsightly droppings deface our public buildings and homes. All in all, there appears to be little that is endearing about this animal.

Pigeons, however, are not without value. Many birding neophytes were introduced to the study of ornithology by learning about the skeleton of the pigeon. To do this they would literally cook the flesh away from the bones and then remount the exposed skeleton on a small wooden plaque. Laboratory experiments also revealed that pigeons can detect colors. An offshoot of this research was the Navy's use of this ability to locate life rafts at sea. The birds were taught to punch a lever with their bill as soon as they spotted a life raft. The success ratio for the pigeons at this task was 90 percent, whereas humans scored only 50 percent. And most of us are aware of pigeons' homing abilities. During both World War I and II pigeons were used to transport secret messages from behind enemy lines. Knowing this, the wily Germans trained Peregrine Falcons to intercept the birds along homing lanes.

MOURNING DOVE

Zenaida macroura

Habitat: Prefers a wide variety of habitats from urban to suburban. Frequents corn and grain fields and local area bird feeding stations.

Local Sites: A familiar backyard bird in the Indianapolis area.

Status: Common resident. During the fall, gathers in flocks of from a few to over one hundred individuals in choice feeding areas. A common visitor to feeding stations.

Length: 12 inches.

Remarks: A familiar sight in most habitats, Mourning Doves do not seem much worse off for the hunting season imposed on them in recent years. Their long, pointed tails, fringed in white, along with their plump bodies and small heads, make them easily separable from all other species of birds in the Indianapolis region. Normally they raise at least two clutches of young per year. The nest is flimsily constructed of small twigs and pine needles and supports two or occasionally three eggs. In fact, the nest is so poorly constructed that many eggs fall through to the ground and are broken. The eggs themselves are a chalky white in color and hatch within thirteen to fourteen days of being laid. Pine stands are a preferred nesting site for this species, although shrubs and deciduous trees are also utilized. During nesting they are ferocious defenders of their nesting territory from other doves; fortunately, they lack adequate armament for this and as a result few real injuries occur.

As with most doves, they feed primarily on seeds and grain found in fields and along road edges. Generally solitary in the nesting season, they form flocks in the fall and winter months at choice feeding locations. At that time of the year they commonly sit on telephone lines and fencerows along the road. Except at feeding stations they form monotypic flocks, seldom mingling with other species. They seem especially prone to disease. As many as 30 percent of the doves that we have banded in suburban areas have been plagued by tumors on their bills, heads, and necks. These tumors do not seem to impair the doves' ability to function normally but do indicate some type of health problem within these populations.

The Mourning Dove's common name comes from its long, soulful call, "oooah-oo-oo-oo," which many non-birders mistake for some species of owl. They call incessantly in the spring, but are normally quiet for the remainder of the year.

YELLOW-BILLED CUCKOO

Coccyzus americanus

Habitat: Open woodland, especially where undergrowth is thick, parks, suburban areas, and scrub.

Local Sites: One of the better areas to observe this bird is the north end of Eagle Creek Park, but it can also be seen about suburban areas with extensive undergrowth.

Status: Fairly common migrant and summer resident, arriving about the first week of May and remaining until the end of September; rarely later. Nests.

Length: 12 inches.

Remarks: Not to be confused with its European counterpart, the Yellow-billed Cuckoo does not give the familiar "cuckoo" call made famous by the clock of the same name. Instead it gives a rather throaty series of "cow" notes that ends in a definite up-raising terminal note—almost as if the bird had the hiccups when finishing its song. It was often called the rain-crow or storm-bird by old-time birders because this species frequently calls before a storm or on gray, overcast days. A closely allied species, the Black-billed Cuckoo, nests only rarely this far south. It differs not only in bill color but in plumage, in that it lacks rusty primaries. Both species are the same size. Another distinction between our cuckoos and the European bird is that both the Yellow-billed and Black-billed Cuckoos are normally nonparasitic. The exception is that on rare occasions, where their territories overlap, one of the cuckoo species will lay its eggs in the nest of the other. Both are exceptionally valuable birds which destroy large numbers of tent caterpillars; indeed, it seems that in years when that pest is particularly abundant, cuckoos are more common.

The nest, which is rather flimsily built, is composed of sticks, vines, and twigs and is often lined with fine grasses. In it the female generally lays from three to four pale greenish eggs, which take about fourteen days to hatch.

EASTERN SCREECH-OWL

Otus asio

Habitat: Mixture of woodlands and fields where the birds have nest sites but where there is sufficient room to hunt. Sometimes found adjacent to suburban areas.

Local Sites: City parks and some suburban areas. Generally difficult to see but frequently heard just after dusk or before dawn.

Status: Fairly common resident. Nests.

Length: 8¹/₂ inches.

Remarks: Our only small "eared" owl, the Eastern Screech-Owl is the commonest owl in our area but is also one of the least seen due to its nocturnal habits and secretive nature. Plumage colors vary from brown to gray to a bright rusty-red, and clutches of young can contain fledglings of all three colors. Eastern Screech-Owls are cavity nesters, utilizing old Northern Flicker holes, woodpecker holes, and man-made nest boxes. This species is most vocal immediately prior to nesting, but many people do not recognize its call as belonging to an owl. It is a long, tremulous whistle, bearing little resemblance to the calls of our other owl species.

The major portion of the Eastern Screech-Owl's diet consists of small rodents such as mice, voles, and shrews, but they will take insects, salamanders, and small snakes when the opportunity presents itself. Like all owls, this species regurgitates the nondigestible parts of its food, the fur and bones, in the form of pellets. Screech-Owl pellets are approximately an inch long and half an inch in diameter, and resemble a cat's furball. These waste products can accumulate into impressive piles under favored feeding perches and are a good way to locate areas in which the species is active. In the winter months these small raptors are frequent automobile casualties as they hunt along roadways. They also suffer predation from the larger species of hawks and owls.

GREAT HORNED OWL

Bubo virginianus

Habitat: Forested areas either deciduous or evergreen and orchards, parks, and brushy areas.

Local Sites: Eagle Creek Park, Atterbury Fish and Wildlife Area, and Morgan-Monroe State Forest. Occasionally found in other parkland areas.

Status: Fairly common resident. Nests.

Length: 22 inches.

Remarks: Ultimate aerial predators, Great Horned Owls will tackle prey up to their own size and considerably heavier. Birds, squirrels, rabbits, raccoons, skunks, and even cats have been discovered dead at nest sites. In years of plenty, these rapacious hunters can be finicky eaters; there are documented cases of their killing large numbers of rodents and consuming only the brains. Great Horned Owls are fearless defenders of their young; on occasion an overinquisitive naturalist has required several hundred stitches to repair the damage done by adult owls on territory. They are not above stealing nest sites and nests from other birds of prey, occasionally killing the rightful owners.

Owl anatomy differs somewhat from that of most birds. Owls have binocular vision and stereo hearing. One disadvantage of binocular vision is the loss of field of view offered by having eyes that are spaced widely apart. Owls cope with this limiting factor by rotating their heads 180 degrees to see behind them. Their eyes are actually larger than a human's, and their aural openings (ears) are the largest of any bird of similar size. These attributes aid in hunting in low light situations by improving depth perception. Owls' feathers are extremely soft, allowing them to make silent approaches on potential prey.

Owls, particularly the Great Horned Owl, figured largely in American Indian folklore and religion. Tribal shamans kept pet owls for guidance and a constant supply of feathers which were considered both good luck and strongly medicinal. Many tribes believed that after death the human spirit came back to earth as an owl. Virtually all primitive cultures associate owls with wisdom, some as evil spirits, others as benefactors willing to impart that wisdom to religious leaders.

BARRED OWL

Strix varia

Habitat: Heavily forested areas, usually along streams or rivers.
Local Sites: The stretch of Fall Creek north of Indianapolis to Geist Reservoir is one of the better places to find this bird. It can also be found at Eagle Creek Park, Atterbury Fish and Wildlife Area, and Morgan-Monroe State Forest.
Status: Fairly common resident. Nests.
Length: 21 inches.
Remarks: With the exception of the radically different and much rarer Barn Owl, the Barred Owl is the only family member in the Indianapolis region with dark brown irises. This species feeds on small rodents, rabbits, squirrels, snakes, and small birds. Year-long residents, they nest in tree cavities as a rule; on rare occasions they will make use of an abandoned hawk or crow nest. Their familiar call, "Who cooks—who cooks for you all," is loud and ringing and can be heard at great distances. Curious and rather tame birds, they are easily enticed close if you imitate their call. They have even been known to come in and investigate when birders "pish" for other species.

We have seen them hunting at dusk around birdbaths, with a lawn sprinkler going full tilt, taking earthworms that were apparently attracted by the wet ground. On cloudy, gray days they often call and hunt throughout the daylight hours. In flight they are powerful, direct fliers with deep wingbeats interspersed with short glides. When sitting they lack the pronounced ear tufts and white throat of the Great Horned Owl.

While this is not the commonest owl in our area, it is probably the one most frequently seen due to its size, habits, and habitat.

NORTHERN SAW-WHET OWL

Aegolius acadicus

Habitat: Dense plantings of conifers, primarily White Pines and Hemlocks. They also occasionally use heavy tangles of grapevines and thick cover when migrating to and from their winter feeding grounds.

Local Sites: The area near the dam on the north side of Geist Reservoir and Atterbury Fish and Wildlife Area in conifer plantings. Rarely found elsewhere in the region.

Status: Very rare winter visitant with few records.

Length: 8 inches.

Remarks: The smallest owl in central Indiana. It lacks the noticeable ear tufts of our region's other small owl, the Eastern Screech-Owl, and is more boldly patterned in browns and white. This delightful little raptor is somewhat cyclic in occurrence. In some winters none are present; in others there are multiple sightings, most of which occur south of the Indianapolis area.

They feed on an assortment of insects, small birds, and rodents. Unfortunately, they frequently fall prey to larger owls and hawks against which their best defense is to remain motionless and hope for the best. Whenever possible they spend the daylight hours inside an old woodpecker hole or natural cavity awaiting dusk when they sally forth in search of sustenance. Extremely tame, they will allow a close approach, in some instances waiting to be touched before taking flight. Even when spooked from a perch they seldom fly more than several hundred feet before coming to rest again. This lack of timidity often results in the birds' demise as roadkills in areas of heavy traffic.

Northern Saw-whet Owls derive their unusual name from their distinctive call, which to some people sounds like someone sharpening a saw blade with a whetstone. They also give a series of repeated monotonous single-note whistles in the spring when courtship begins. Even when calling continuously, however, these tiny warriors can be exceedingly difficult to locate because of the ventriloquial effect that the call produces.

COMMON NIGHTHAWK

Chordeiles minor

Habitat: Urban and suburban areas with extensive gravel-topped buildings upon which they nest. In migration they can be seen hawking insects over farm fields and in towns.

Local Sites: Downtown Indianapolis and in other areas locally where nest sites can be found. During migration they can be seen hawking insects in the searchlights of the Soldiers' and Sailors' Monument downtown.

Status: Fairly common resident and migrant whose numbers seem to be decreasing. Arrives about the first week of May and remains until the first week of October. Some fall migrations in September are quite noticeable, as the birds can be seen flying overhead. Nests.

Length: $9^1/_2$ inches.

Remarks: In spite of the name and a general superficial resemblance, Common Nighthawks are not really members of the hawk family but belong to a widespread group of birds known as nightjars. (The Whip-Poor-Will is also a nightjar.) In less enlightened times rural people referred to nightjars as "goatsuckers," believing that they came into farmyards to steal milk from their goats. Members of this family are characterized by their falcon-like shapes in flight, short bills, and crepuscular or nocturnal habits. Nighthawks are most active at dusk, when they can be seen pursuing insects in large open areas with their rapid, erratic, and highly acrobatic flight. Even though they are short-billed, their mouths are quite large, enabling them to literally hit their dinner on the wing.

The Common Nighthawk normally nests on gravel-topped buildings and rarely in scrapes made on the ground. The courtship display is quite spectacular, with a male bird ascending to considerable height, closing his wings against his body, and diving down toward the female. When he does so, the air rushing through the feathers of the bird, with the ascent at the last moment, creates a booming noise that is audible from some distance away.

Common Nighthawks are the only one of the family likely to be seen during daylight hours, and can be found in urban settings as readily as in rural ones.

CHIMNEY SWIFT

Chaetura pelagica

Habitat: Open areas and woodland around human habitation; nests and roosts primarily in chimneys.

Local Sites: A familiar bird in central Indiana, especially near homes and buildings with large chimneys.

Status: Common summer resident, arriving in April and departing about mid-October.

Length: 5¼ inches.

Remarks: America's foremost ornithologist, Roger Tory Peterson, the originator of the famed Field Guide series, called this bird "a cigar with wings," and that is exactly what it looks like as it flies through the sky. Interestingly, this bird's winter home was a mystery for many years. Arthur Cleveland Bent wrote in 1940, in his classic Life History studies, that the bird wintered at some as yet undiscovered location in South America. The mystery was reported to have been solved, however, when an ornithologist visiting Peru noted that one of the necklaces an Indian was wearing contained a number of bird bands that had been taken from this species high up in the Andes.

The Chimney Swift gets its name from its habit of building a nest and rearing its young in chimneys. Before the settlers arrived, the birds used hollow trees. The nest, made of small twigs that are gathered in full flight, is attached to the chimney using a glutinous saliva that hardens when exposed to air. (In Borneo, natives collect a closely allied species' nest to use in the epicurean delight known as bird's nest soup.) The female lays from three to six glossy white eggs that take about eighteen to twenty-one days to hatch.

In the fall, migrating chimney swifts gather in huge flocks, sometimes numbering into the thousands, and roost communally in large chimneys. Flocks of birds can be seen toward dusk, flying erratically around these roost sites. Just before dark they will descend into the chimneys to spend the night.

RUBY-THROATED HUMMINGBIRD

Archilochus colubris

Habitat: Mixed woodland, secondary growth, parks, and open situations with scattered trees. Forages in meadows and gardens.

Local Sites: The nature center at Eagle Creek Park has a garden specifically designed to attract hummers. The bird is also widely found wherever there is an abundance of flowers (especially red ones) and is attracted to sugar water placed in appropriate feeders near homes.

Status: Common migrant and summer resident. Nests. Arrives in late April and normally remains until the end of September. Where feeding conditions are optimum some birds stay later, into October.

Length: 3³/₄ inches.

Remarks: The famous European ornithologist and painter John Gould, who wrote and illustrated (in part) the magnificent folio on the world's hummingbirds, saw his first wild one in 1857 and recorded this experience in words of great delight. No doubt this species was among those he saw. In the Indianapolis area, however, the Ruby-throat is the only member of the family normally seen—a mere mite of a bird whose small size, much of which is bill, is more likely confused at first glance with some insect. The male bird sports an iridescent, reddish throat which appears black unless seen in good light, while the female resembles the male but lacks this throat mark.

The unique courtship display is among the marvels of the bird world. We have witnessed it at Eagle Creek Park. The male buzzes a feeding female in a series of arcs much like a pendulum, all the while twittering and chirping as if hoping to attract her attention. In late May the female builds a delicate nest out of plant down, small fibers, and bud scales which she attaches to a limb with spider silk. The interior of this nest is lined with lichens, after which two eggs are laid. Although this is a rather small clutch, in good years the species is double-brooded. Rearing the young is left up to the female; she will not tolerate male birds in the vicinity of the nest.

Hummingbirds can often be attracted to your yard with plantings of columbine, bee balm, fuchsia, trumpet vine, jewelweed, and hollyhock. Along with honey bees, the ruby-throat is a prime source of pollination; its frequent visits from flower to flower help ensure the future of some of our flowering plants and trees. To further entice hummers, a mixture of one part sugar to four parts of water will prove attractive, but be sure to remove the feeders before the middle of October; otherwise, there is a chance that the birds may become dependent upon this source of easy food and be tempted not to migrate before freezing weather.

BELTED KINGFISHER

Ceryle alcyon

Habitat: Frequents rivers, streams, fish hatcheries, and lakes.
Local Sites: Is seen along all the water courses in the Indianapolis area, but seems to prefer the smaller streams or creeks.
Status: Common summer resident. Nests. Some birds remain as long as there is open water in the winter. During severe winters most birds retreat as far south as open water, only to reappear again when mild weather returns. There are those rare occasions, however, when some birds are caught by a sudden drop in the temperature and perish.
Length: 13 inches.
Remarks: The loud, rattling call often heard along waterways comes from this handsome member of the kingfisher family, the only one found in our region. Although much maligned by fishermen because of its propensity to take fish, the truth of the matter is that most of those taken are not game fish but small fries and minnows, hardly what one would consider of interest to the angler. This is one of the few species of birds in which the female sports brighter colors than her male counterpart. The female has not only the bluish band across the chest but a russet one as well, just below it, giving her a more dapper appearance than the male bird. Both birds exhibit a large, showy crest and a somewhat massive beak. The latter is an apt adaptation for its role as a fisherman *par excellence.*

When fishing, this bird sometimes hovers over the water and then quickly dives with a loud splash, usually emerging with a struggling fish. At other times it can be noticed perched over the water, peering intently downward, waiting for the next meal to show up.

Kingfishers nest in holes excavated in the banks that border our waterways. Sometimes these holes are about three feet from the top of the bank and extend slightly upward some three to nine feet, rarely fifteen feet. Here the five to eight whitish eggs are laid with hatching occurring from twenty-three to twenty-four days later.

RED-HEADED WOODPECKER

Melanerpes erythrocephalus

Habitat: Open woodland areas with a predominance of beech or oak trees. Found in parks, orchards, and especially along roadsides.

Local Sites: City parks and small woodlots. Can frequently be found along roadsides, perched upon telephone poles and fence posts.

Status: Uncommon migrant and summer resident. Nests. In good foraging areas birds may remain throughout the winter, particularly if the beech mast crop is good. Formerly more abundant. Frequents suet feeders.

Length: 9$^{1}/_{2}$ inches.

Remarks: The flashing black and white wingpatches and blazing red head make the Red-headed Woodpecker one of the most visible denizens of central Indiana. Unfortunately, it is not as common as it was years ago when each beech tree woodlot was sure to have several pairs of this attractive bird. It is thought that their propensity for frequenting roadsides is the primary cause for this decline in numbers. Birds are attracted to waste grain scattered along the road, and when flushed are not quick enough to dodge a passing vehicle.

Red-heads can be quite pugnacious at feeders, driving away other species and even successfully taking on the larger Pileated Woodpecker. They often raid fruit trees, much to the frustration of the owner, but the overall good that they do in eliminating some of the wood-boring insects more than makes up for this annoying trait. Like other members of the genus they have a tendency to store nuts in cavities and knot holes of trees. Some even resort to placing them between the shingles of roofs or driving them into railroad ties.

All woodpeckers advertise their territory by drumming, using a variety of sites from galvanized tin roofs to telephone poles. For some time in the 1950s, near downtown Indianapolis, a bird gave out with this loud tattoo from a metal telephone post, much to the consternation of nearby residents.

RED-BELLIED WOODPECKER

Melanerpes carolinus

Habitat: Parks, suburban areas interspersed with trees, and orchards.
Local Sites: Eagle Creek Park, Atterbury Fish and Wildlife Area, suburban areas with feeding stations, and most city parks.
Status: Common resident. Nests. Much more abundant than thirty years ago, as species seems to be in a range expansion.
Length: $9^1/_4$ inches.
Remarks: Back in the late 1940s this bird was rare in Indianapolis and birders would consider it a choice find on one of their outings; today they seem to be prospering, with pairs of birds noted in most city parks. Frequent visitors to bird feeders, they will eat oil sunflower seeds as well as suet.

The long, flexible tongues of woodpeckers, which in some species can be extended four inches, are well adapted for extracting larvae. Other anatomical modifications include powerful muscles in the neck, a thick skull, and broad, shock-absorbing ribs. These characteristics, along with a chisel-like beak, make woodpeckers superb wood-boring animals.

All woodpeckers sometimes store food for later consumption. Red-bellied Woodpeckers have been noted placing poison ivy berries and whole or fragmented acorns deep in crannies or crevices of trees for later use. These are apparently beyond the reach of surface-feeding birds like titmice and chickadees.

Often called the Zebra Woodpecker, the Red-belly is an attractive bird with its alternate, horizontal black and white stripes running from the back of the neck to the rump. This feature is a much better field mark than the hard-to-see reddish belly. In the male bird the red on the head extends from the base of the bill over the eye and down to the back of the neck. The female's head is quite similar, except that the red does not extend all the way to the bill.

They lay their three to five white eggs at the base of excavated holes in a variety of different tree species, most generally in old decayed stumps. The period of incubation is about fourteen days.

DOWNY WOODPECKER
Picoides pubescens

Habitat: Utilizes a wide variety of habitats to feed. We have seen them industriously pounding on old cattail stalks in the middle of a marsh and out in cornfields searching for food on standing corn, as well as in their usual haunts, the woodlands.
Local Sites: City parks and both urban and suburban areas. Comes freely to feeding stations.
Status: Common resident. Breeds.
Length: $6^3/_4$ inches.
Remarks: These little birds are smartly patterned in white and black with the male having a touch of red on the back of the head, accentuating the pied plumage. As with all other woodpeckers the Downy's tail feathers are very stiff and serve as support when the bird is hammering away in search of the insects and larvae that constitute its food supply.

The Downy Woodpecker makes its nest in dead or dying trees, carving out an excavation with an entrance hole about the size of a quarter. Nest heights vary widely but are generally within thirty feet of the ground. Very similar to the related Hairy Woodpecker, the Downy is about one and three-quarter inches smaller and has a proportionately smaller bill. The call of the Downy is higher pitched and less strident than that of its larger relative, and its drumming is more rapid.

They sometimes begin courting in late winter, when the male and female can be seen in apparent pursuit of one another, rapidly ascending or descending a tree or flying in small bounds with a flight similar to that of American Goldfinches. At this time of the year they are quite noisy, producing a variety of calls and considerable drumming. Because of the number of wood-boring insects they take, you can consider yourself lucky if you have a pair of these birds near.

NORTHERN FLICKER
Colaptes auratus

Habitat: Parks, open areas interspersed with trees. Both urban and suburban areas.

Local Sites: Found in a wide variety of sites in the Indianapolis region, from backyards to city parks, woodlands, and river valleys.

Status: Common summer resident. Nests. Most birds migrate out of the area and to some extent may be replaced by other more northern birds during mild winters.

Length: 12^1/$_2$ inches.

Remarks: Northern Flickers are called Yellowhammers in many parts of the south because of their bright golden-yellow underwing feathers and because many of the first European immigrants remembered a bird with similar coloration, so named, from their native countries. A member of the woodpecker family, it is the only one seen habitually feeding on the ground. Catching worms and ants are two favorite pastimes of this medium-sized woodpecker. It has been estimated that as much as 78 percent of the insects taken by flickers consist of various ant species, more than any other species of North American bird.

Normally solitary when nesting, they form loose flocks during the spring and fall migration, up to two dozen birds in a group. Flickers are somewhat different from other woodpeckers in their selection of nest sites. For the most part they excavate their own nest cavities, but they are not above using abandoned woodpecker holes or natural or man-made cavities. Nests have been located in old haystacks, drainpipes, kingfisher burrows, and on several occasions out in the open on the ground.

In the not too distant past flickers were considered fair game for the sportsman, and this so-called Partridge Woodpecker was cherished as prize table fare. The cessation of songbird hunting has put an end to that threat; now the worst enemy of the flicker is probably the European Starling. Starlings not only compete for food but utilize many of the same nest sites, frequently evicting flickers from their nests.

PILEATED WOODPECKER

Dryocopus pileatus

Habitat: Heavily wooded areas in stream or river valleys or adjacent to lakes.

Local Sites: Eagle Creek Park, Geist Reservoir, Atterbury Fish and Wildlife Area, Walnut Grove in Shelby County, and Morgan-Monroe State Forest. Has been seen in the Broad Ripple area and northern Indianapolis and was recently found in the southern part of the city near Southport and Waverly.

Status: Fairly common resident. Nests.

Length: 16¹/₂ inches.

Remarks: Our largest woodpecker and only slightly smaller than the American Crow, the Pileated is a true conservation success story. Forty years ago they were unknown in Indianapolis but now can be found with some frequency. When present they can easily be detected by their loud, piercing calls and the tell-tale holes that they carve into trees for nests and in search of food. As with most woodpeckers, they feed largely on insects, worms, and grubs chiseled out of dead or diseased trees. Strikingly patterned in white and black with a pronounced crest, these magnificent birds look quite handsome as they fly and forage about in old second growth deciduous forest. They are seldom found far from good-sized stands of large trees, which makes them susceptible to decline in areas where logging occurs regularly. Somewhat wary in other circumstances, in harsh weather they will patronize feeding stations, preferring peanut butter or suet to any other offerings.

The sexes are very similar in appearance. The only noticeable difference is in the coloration of the whisker-mark—red in males, black in females. Pileateds are strong fliers and demonstrate the typical undulating flight of all woodpeckers—strong flaps interspersed with short glides. Their drumming pattern is readily separated from that of other woodpeckers because of its slow, methodical cadence.

EASTERN WOOD-PEWEE

Contopus virens

Habitat: Forest, woodland, scrub, parks, and open situations with scattered trees. Breeds in deciduous forest and forest edge and in open woodland.

Local Sites: Eagle Creek Park, Holliday Park, along White River in northern Indianapolis, Geist Reservoir, Atterbury Fish and Wildlife Area, Walnut Grove, and Morgan-Monroe State Forest.

Status: Fairly common summer resident, although in recent years it seems to be in a decline. Nests. Arrives about the first week of May and remains until mid- to late September.

Length: 6¼ inches.

Remarks: The day's heat can become oppressive toward the end of July; at times the air seems so thick that you can cut it with a knife. This is the season of the annual cicada, those nasty, ever-present yellow jackets, and the incessant, questioning song of the Red-eyed Vireo. Deep in the woods, a nondescript olive-greenish bird sallies forth from some exposed dead branch to snatch a small insect that passes by too closely. Upon returning to its perch it gobbles down its prize and calls forth a plaintive yet far-reaching "pee-a-wee." You have just encountered an interesting member of the flycatcher family—the Eastern Wood-Pewee, one of the few species that habitually sing throughout the summer and usually for most of the day.

Wood-Pewees set up housekeeping in some of the more heavily wooded areas about town. Here they build their nest anywhere from fifteen to sixty-five feet high on some small limb, typically far from the trunk, and the female lays from two to four eggs in a dainty, shallow, thick-walled cup of grasses, weeds, fibers, spider webs, and hair. Incubation takes from twelve to thirteen days.

WILLOW FLYCATCHER

Empidonax traillii

Habitat: Lightly wooded areas with many small trees and shrubs and some nearby water source, particularly swampy thickets of willow or buttonbush.

Local Sites: The coffer dam at Eagle Creek Reservoir behind the nature center annually holds from one to two pairs. Atterbury Fish and Wildlife Area. Formerly Geist Reservoir, before it was heavily developed.

Status: Fairly common summer resident. Breeds. Arrives in early May and remains until late September.

Length: 5³/₄ inches.

Remarks: A member of the genus of difficult to identify flycatchers known as Empidonaxes, the Willow Flycatcher is perhaps the most common member of that group in central Indiana. Helpful in identification is their distinctive call, likened to "fitz-bew," and their habitat selection, although the latter cannot always be considered definitive.

Their nests are generally placed within fifteen feet of the ground and are constructed of a mixture of grasses, animal hairs, spider webs, or any other fibrous material that the birds can garner. Because of the materials they use, the nests on occasion have long trailers of filaments hanging down.

Two separate species, the Alder and the Willow, were at one time considered to be one species—the supposed Traill's Flycatcher. They have recently been separated on the basis of call notes, habitat, and geographic differences, the Alder being more northerly in distribution and only a migrant in the Indianapolis region.

EASTERN PHOEBE

Sayornis phoebe

Habitat: Found in open areas, especially near culverts, bridges, and shelter houses, where the bird frequently nests. In migration, can occur about thickets, city parks, and suburban sites.

Local Sites: Eagle Creek Park, Holliday Park, Atterbury Fish and Wildlife Area.

Status: Fairly common summer resident; very rare in the winter. Arrives in early March and remains until mid-December or as long as weather permits.

Length: 7 inches.

Remarks: The Eastern Phoebe has the honor of being the first banded bird in North America. John James Audubon, the famous naturalist and documenter of early American birdlife, attached small silver threads to the legs of a pair of nesting phoebes near his home in Pennsylvania during the breeding season. The following year he noted the banded pair back at the original nesting site, thus proving that this particular pair had returned to the area.

During the nesting season they seem to like the close proximity of humans; they often build their nests beneath shelter houses where the beams join at the corner, or on top of a light fixture, or beneath a bridge. The latter location is frequently used in the Indianapolis area. At Eagle Creek Park for a number of years a pair consistently used the inside of an abandoned barn just south of the nature center, until the barn collapsed. The nest consists of weeds, grasses and mud into which three to six white eggs are laid. Incubation is done by the female alone and generally takes fifteen to sixteen days. According to the literature, this species is heavily parasitized by the Brown-headed Cowbird; the phoebe will often abandon a nest if the cowbird lays its eggs first.

Eastern Phoebes have a habit of pumping their tail upon landing; this and the constant call note, which mimics its name, are useful field marks.

GREAT CRESTED FLYCATCHER

Myiarchus crinitus

Habitat: Forests, parks, orchards, and wooded stream valleys.
Local Sites: This species is generally fairly easy to find in any of the wooded city parks and along both White River and Fall Creek in northern Indianapolis. It can also be found in a wide variety of sites in the central Indiana area.
Status: Common summer resident. Breeds. Arrives about mid-April and remains until September.
Length: 8 inches.
Remarks: Toward the end of April when the dogwoods and the red-buds begin to bloom, if a handsome, medium-sized, crested bird makes its presence known by calling with a loud, penetrating "weep-weep-weep," it is the Great Crested Flycatcher, just returned from its winter home in Central and northern South America. It is a noisy bird at this time of the year, calling continuously as if to announce to the world that this particular location is to be the site of its summer

home. Here it will build its nest in some abandoned woodpecker hole or furnished nest box where the female will lay from four to eight brownish speckled eggs. The nest is a curious affair of twigs, leaves, hair, and feathers, and often a discarded snakeskin, which some ornithologists formerly believed was a survival tactic to ward off potential predators. There is, however, no substantive proof that this is the case; it is more probable that the birds merely use this material to add to the nest's bulk. After nesting season the birds become rather quiet before they leave for their winter homes once again.

A rather sedentary bird, like other members of the flycatcher family it often perches in some exposed area for long periods of time. It can be easily observed as it alternately dashes off to catch some flying insect and then returns to the perch. Because they take large numbers of noxious insects, they are among our most beneficial birds and should be encouraged to inhabit our orchards, gardens, and woodlands.

EASTERN KINGBIRD

Tyrannus tyrannus

Habitat: Orchards, parks, and rather open areas with adjacent trees and scrub.
Local Sites: Eagle Creek Park, particularly the north end and around the ice-skating ponds. Several pairs annually use Atterbury Fish and Wildlife Area.
Status: Fairly common summer resident. Breeds. Arrives about mid-April and leaves about the last week of August or the first week of September.
Length: 8$^1/_2$ inches.
Remarks: The Eastern Kingbird is one of the largest flycatchers in central Indiana, and certainly the most conspicuous. It is most often seen sitting alongside roads on telephone wires or fences in open country. They are noisy, aggressive birds and will often harass larger birds such as crows, hawks, and owls when their territory is invaded.

The nest is a cupped affair made out of fine grasses, twine, and animal hair and is usually located in a small tree or shrub less than twenty feet off the ground. Adult birds frequently sit in the tops of much taller trees, surveying their domain for intruders or prey, and feeding on flying insects, which they snatch out of the air with considerable dispatch. Beekeepers find them to be somewhat of a nuisance, since once a hive is found they will take up residence near this convenient source of nourishment and are usually very reluctant to depart for less favorable hunting grounds.

HORNED LARK

Eremophila alpestris

Habitat: Open fields, especially newly plowed. Frequently seen along roadsides, feeding on scattered grain.

Local Sites: The open fields just west of Eagle Creek Reservoir and near the entrance of Atterbury Fish and Wildlife Area. Frequently found in the farm fields of Shelby County and at other open situations.

Status: Common resident. Local populations are augmented in winter by birds which migrate to this area.

Length: 7¼ inches.

Remarks: At least two races of the Horned Lark, both the same size, can be found in central Indiana in the winter. The paler race, called the Prairie Horned Lark, has a buff throat and immaculate white eyeline. The so-called Northern Horned Lark has a yellowish throat and eyeline. While they do have "horns"—actually small tufts of feathers—these are very difficult to discern except at extreme close range.

They nest in March, on the ground, often in quite exposed areas. The nest itself is a well-defined cup of grasses and animal hairs and normally contains four eggs. As with most ground nesting species, both eggs and young suffer heavily from predation from skunks and raccoons. For most of the year Horned Larks are omnivorous, feeding on seeds, grain, and insects, but in winter they become wholly dependent on weed seeds and leftover grain.

Horned Larks are the most common bird in their chosen habitat and are usually seen in pairs except in the fall and winter, when groups of several hundred birds can often be seen. Snow Buntings and Lapland Longspurs often associate with these flocks, so look such groups over well. They are Holarctic in distribution—that is, they are distributed over the North Pole into Europe—and in Europe are known to birdwatchers as Shore Larks.

PURPLE MARTIN

Progne subis

Habitat: Large open areas, frequently near water. Nests in tree holes and bird houses.

Local Sites: Widely found in central Indiana, in particular where special martin houses are placed in open areas to attract them. In migration, often congregates in large flocks.

Status: Fairly common, but not as common as forty years ago. Male scouts arrive early in March. Martins begin migrating south in August, and by the first of September most birds are gone.

Length: 8 inches.

Remarks: Purple Martins are one of America's favorite birds, and it would be hard to find someone who has not at least heard of them. Much of their notoriety began in the mid-1960s in a small Illinois town by the name of Griggsville, where martins were suggested as a natural method of insect control because of their supposed ability to eat over ten thousand small flying insects, like flies and mosquitoes, per day. The governor of Illinois once issued a proclamation designating a "Purple Martin Day," and on one occasion this species sparked a heated debate in the Illinois General Assembly: some members advocated making it the state bird, displacing the Northern Cardinal. There is even a drink called a "Purple Martini," and a movie has been made about the birds.

Purple Martins are easily attracted to nest houses that are placed in appropriate habitat. Martin colonies can range in size from one to over a hundred pairs of birds and, since they are in no way detrimental to man, it is common to see houses put out by people who otherwise take little interest in birds.

Martins have very large mouths and can hit a flying insect with ease while on the wing. The long, pointed, back-swept wings make them fast and maneuverable fliers.

TREE SWALLOW

Tachycineta bicolor

Habitat: Open areas near water. Nests in trees with holes over water. Also uses bluebird nest boxes.
Local Sites: Eagle Creek Reservoir and Stone Arch Lake at Atterbury Fish and Wildlife Area.
Status: Fairly common summer resident. Breeds. Arrives early in March and remains until the last week of October.
Length: 5³/₄ inches.
Remarks: These smartly plumed little birds are glossy, metallic blue-green above and snow-white below. Soon after appearing in the spring they begin searching for suitable nest sites—waterways with old, standing trees that have cavities in which the swallows can raise their young. They will also nest in man-made boxes placed in the appropriate habitat and frequently usurp bluebird boxes that are positioned near water. The nest itself is lined with breast feathers from the adults, and it is not uncommon to see them near nesting areas, carrying these feathers around in their bills. The usual clutch is four to five eggs of a milky white color, which hatch in June, with young departing the nest by late July.

NORTHERN ROUGH-WINGED SWALLOW

Stelgidopteryx serripennis

Habitat: Steams, rivers, lakes and reservoirs. Nests in culverts, holes in banks, old tile, and drainpipes of bridges.
Local Sites: Perhaps the most widely distributed of all the swallow species in central Indiana, occurring in a wide variety of areas where there is water.
Status: Common summer resident. Breeds. Arrives about the third week of April and remains until about the end of August or first part of September.
Length: 5¹/₂ inches.
Remarks: With a name almost as long as the birds themselves, Northern Rough-winged Swallows are common near water and nest

in steep sand banks and the drainpipes of bridges, which they tend to use year after year. Many times they simply conscript an abandoned kingfisher burrow rather than going to the trouble of excavating their own. Far back in the tunnels they lay two to three white eggs which hatch in sixteen days. Unlike Bank Swallows, pairs rarely nest colonially. They do not really construct a nest as such, simply lining a slight depression with feathers. During migration they are abundant, but numbers decline somewhat as the nesting season sets in; many proceed to areas farther north to breed. As is the case with all of our local swallows, Rough-wings are voracious insectivores, devouring thousands of flying insects daily.

This is the plainest member of the family in North America, but it makes up for that by having a personality all its own. During the spring migration it is not uncommon to see thousands of individuals of this species in mixed swallow flocks on large bodies of water. It is impressive to watch such a large number of birds engaged in high-speed, sophisticated aerobatics as they play and feed close to the water's surface. They often skim insects from the top of the water as they feed in much the same manner as a Black Tern.

BANK SWALLOW

Riparia riparia

Habitat: A colonial nesting species that uses steep river or lake banks and especially gravel pits.
Local Sites: A colony nested for several years in the waterfowl resting area in back of the nature center at Eagle Creek Park. Some of the gravel pits south of Indianapolis are still used.
Status: Locally common summer resident. Breeds. Arrives about mid-April and departs in late August.
Length: $5^{1}/_{4}$ inches.
Remarks: Easily distinguished from all of the other swallows in central Indiana by its snow-white underparts, interrupted by a narrow dark brown chest band, and its brown back. It nests in steep gravel riverbanks and gravel pit spoils where there may be as many as several hundred burrows to a colony. In prime nesting locations, these bur-

rows may be spaced only inches apart. The colonies are revisited year after year but often require considerable renovation before they are serviceable once again. Away from the colonies these social little birds can be difficult to locate during the summer months.

As with the Northern Rough-winged Swallow, not much of a nest is constructed, merely a shallow depression, lined with feathers. Two or three white eggs are laid that hatch within fifteen days. Young Bank Swallows are out and flying within a month of hatching and closely resemble the adult birds. Bank Swallows are prodigious insectivores, like all swallows, and can be seen hawking flying insects low over the water's surface. When actively engaged in migration, however, they fly at considerable heights where the winds are more favorable and predictable. Their call is a low, unmelodic buzz, reminiscent of some type of insect rather than a bird, that is most frequently given in flight. Holarctic in distribution, they are referred to by the European birdwatching community as Sand Martins even though they are considerably smaller than the Purple Martin.

BARN SWALLOW

Hirundo rustica

Habitat: Frequently seen near open farm land, golf courses, sod farms, and agricultural areas. In migration with other swallow species.
Local Sites: Just about every fair-sized barn has numbers of this bird, nesting both inside and outside. Nests are sometimes built under rafters or where cross-beams join.
Status: Common summer resident. Breeds. Arrives in mid-April and leaves about the first of October.
Length: 6³/₄ inches.
Remarks: To our eyes, this is the most colorful and sleek of all the swallows. With its steel-blue back and upper wing coverts, buffy underparts, and white-spotted, deeply forked tail it is unlikely to be confused with any of the other North American swallow species. It is longer than any of the other swallows except the much heavier Purple Martin, but this is largely due to the length of the Barn Swallow's slender tail, which makes it appear slimmer in flight than other mem-

bers of the family. Its call, mostly given in flight, is a prolonged, high-pitched twittering.

Nesting commences in June with the nest being constructed out of mud and affixed to the underside of a bridge or to a building—often a barn, hence the bird's name. The nest is deeply cupped and lined with fine grass and feathers and usually contains three or four eggs that are milky white in color. The young hatch in three weeks and are able to fly in approximately three weeks more.

Barn Swallows take flying insects on the wing with remarkable dispatch and on occasion will scoop insects off the water's surface. In the fall, as with other swallow species, they tend to form large flocks that at times can be quite impressive as they move through our region.

BLUE JAY

Cyanocitta cristata

Habitat: Inhabits a wide variety of habitat from coniferous and deciduous forests to urban and suburban areas. Comes freely to feeding stations.
Local Sites: The Blue Jay is one of the more conspicuous birds nearly everywhere.
Status: Common resident; some more northern populations migrate through during April and again in October. Nests.
Length: 11 inches.
Remarks: When we think of the Blue Jay we always think of Easter. When that season rolls around we scatter the remnants of what the Easter bunny has left at our house and the jays come *en masse*. The bird certainly does like eggshells. This propensity for eating eggs often gets the jay into trouble: many suspect that the bird is nothing more than a thief, robbing other birds' nests and disrupting their households. In truth, studies conducted by leading ornithologists reveal that only a small percentage of wild birds' eggs are eaten. A large portion of jays' diet consists of beetles, grasshoppers, caterpillars, and varied vegetable and fruity foods like acorns, wheat, oats, sumac, currants, blackberries, wild grapes, and hawthorn. We suspect that when the jays eat eggshells they do so to obtain some mineral necessary for their diet.

They are handsome birds with a perky topknot and striking blue, white, and black plumage. On a cold, overcast winter's day when the snow lies deep around the bird feeders this species and the Northern Cardinal are a contrast in color with their plumage seeming to dazzle against the gray and white background.

Although it is normally considered a permanent resident there seem to be two populations, one that migrates through the Indianapolis area and one that remains all year. During these migratory periods the jays can be easily seen as they wing their way across the sky, usually following some river valley or natural outcrop.

Like all members of the crow family they have a habit of harassing hawks and owls, mobbing the birds and forcing them to take flight. It is a good bet that if you hear a lot of jays or crows they are engaged in such activity.

For whatever reason some people dislike the bird, it seems to be a highly adaptable species and one that will remain part of our avifauna for a long time.

AMERICAN CROW

Corvus brachyrhynchos

Habitat: Inhabits a wide variety of habitat, from open woodland to agricultural areas and suburban locales.

Local Sites: Easily found nearly everywhere. Some birds were seen in downtown Indianapolis in the old outdoor market and flying to and from their roosting sites.

Status: Common resident. Breeds. Local populations augmented by birds from farther north during the winter.

Length: 17$\frac{1}{2}$ inches.

Remarks: Crows are familiar to almost everyone. Large and jet black, they are highly vocal and utilize virtually every habitat within their range. Crows are also exceptionally intelligent. A friend of ours kept a crow as a pet for many years and had it trained to speak and do tricks. "Joe" the crow would ask for either ice cream or tea, depending upon his current mood, and would even wish you a good morning or tell you goodbye, whichever was pertinent at the time.

Considered a pest by farmers, crows probably do more good by eating harmful insects and rodents than they do harm by damaging crops. They eat just about anything that comes their way—insects, rodents, small birds, eggs, fish, reptiles, and amphibians are all fair game—but technically they are not predators. Crows will team up to rob other birds of their prey, one distracting the rightful owner (often it sneaks around behind the victim and pulls its tail until it turns to defend itself), while another snatches the goods. Carrion is also a major part of their diet; they can quite often be seen sitting alongside the highway feasting on road-killed animals. You may even find them frequenting fast-food parking lots. Farm crops make up a very small portion of the food consumed.

Crows form "cooperative groups" when breeding, a strategy designed to help guard eggs and young against potential predators. Mobbing behavior is exhibited against any hawk or owl that could be perceived as a threat to the group. Large terrestrial mammals are not exempt from these attacks: coyotes, dogs, racoons, and even people have been mobbed for approaching nests too closely. In winter in the Indianapolis area, up until the mid-1960s, crows used to form immense roosts composed of thousands of birds. Breaking into smaller groups to forage by day, they regrouped at dusk and literally filled the trees for acres around. Now these roosts, some of which had been used for years, have been disbanded into smaller, more compact units.

CAROLINA CHICKADEE

Parus carolinensis

Habitat: Woodland, clearings and edge, second growth woodland, parks, and urban and suburban areas.
Local Sites: Fairly well distributed in central Indiana and a familiar bird at feeding stations and city parks.
Status: Common resident. Breeds.
Length: 4³/₄ inches.
Remarks: If one were to take a poll of favorite backyard birds Carolina Chickadees would probably rank very high, for they are trusting

little birds that come eagerly to our feeders for handouts all year long. Sporting black caps and chins along with grayish overall plumage, they appear quite dapper. This, coupled with their energetic movements and appealing countenances, places them high on everybody's list. Often confused with the larger and more northerly Black-capped Chickadee, they can only be told from that species by means of call notes and very indistinct field marks. The Black-cap, however, is a much rarer bird here, appearing only during severe winters and then only for a short period of time.

Carolina Chickadees are among the first birds to appear at a feeder in the morning, and if by chance that feeder is empty, they promptly let you know, scolding you with a sharp "chick-a-dee-dee-dee." They nest in a variety of locations—old hollow metal fence posts, rotting stumps, and occasionally nest boxes—but they usually prefer rotting stumps. Both sexes excavate some five to six inches deep in the soft wood, and here the female lays five to eight eggs, which hatch about thirteen days later. To see a family of chickadees is a delightful sight. The babies, miniature editions of their parents, line up on some small branch where they eagerly beg for food with much noise and wing quivering.

At feeders they particularly like oil sunflower seeds, and if you desire to see them at their best then mount a small plexiglass feeder next to or on your window. Here you will be entertained through many a stormy winter day with the antics of one of the most engaging birds in central Indiana.

TUFTED TITMOUSE

Parus bicolor

Habitat: Woodland, open areas with scattered trees, city parks, and suburban areas.

Local Sites: Indianapolis city parks and suburbs. Found nearly everywhere there is a good stand of trees.

Status: Common resident. Breeds.

Length: 6¹/₂ inches.

Remarks: These active birds with their jaunty crests and engaging demeanor are frequent visitors to bird feeders. They are most evident in early spring when courting males can be heard giving their repetitious "peter-peter" songs. Inquisitive birds, they can easily be enticed with "pishing" sounds to approach the observer; when thus attracted, they gaze at the intruder with beady black eyes and jump from twig to twig, all the while uttering a harsh, grating call reminiscent of the Carolina Chickadee's.

The female bird lays her four to eight whitish eggs at the bottom of a tree cavity located anywhere from two to as high as eighty feet, with incubation taking approximately twelve to thirteen days. The birds use a variety of materials to line the nest: string, bark chips, and even hair taken from a man's head or beard. Like other members of their family, young titmice greatly resemble the adults. The young birds often perch, all in a row, on a small twig, waiting for the parents to bring them some choice morsel or seed. After the nesting season, when the birds become silent, they can be difficult to see amid the foliage of the trees. Titmice and other small birds will often mob an Eastern Screech-Owl, causing that bird to snap its beak and occasionally flushing it.

During the winter, when not at the feeders, small family groups roam through the woods in company with chickadees and kinglets in search of food. They like to glean small grubs and insects from beneath the bark of trees.

WHITE-BREASTED NUTHATCH

Sitta carolinensis

Habitat: Deciduous or coniferous woods and partly open areas with scattered trees.
Local Sites: Indianapolis city parks and suburban areas. Frequently comes to feeding stations.
Status: Common resident. Breeds.
Length: $5^3/_4$ inches.
Remarks: Nuthatches are one of the few species of birds in Indiana that consistently go down the trunks of trees head first, behavior that helps a great deal in identifying them. Like woodpeckers, they have extremely stiff tail feathers which they use for props as they explore

under the bark of trees for the insects that make up their diet. Smaller than any of our woodpeckers, they do not compete with that group of birds but prefer to glean insects off trees rather than probing into the wood as woodpeckers do. The White-breasted Nuthatch frequently visits feeding stations, readily eating sunflower seeds or suet. Although it is common during the breeding season, populations increase with the onset of fall as migrants from farther north swell the local ranks. With their blue-gray backs, black caps, and white underparts, they appear quite dapper but a bit chunkier than the Red-breasted Nuthatch, which is less commonly seen in Indiana.

Nuthatches are among those birds that mob and scold small raptors in defense of their territories. On one occasion a Northern Saw-whet Owl was discovered when several nuthatches of both species excitedly surrounded it, scolding loudly in a vain attempt to drive it off. Uttering their distinctive "yank-yank-yank," they maintained a discreet distance but continued to harass the owl for the better part of an hour before going on to other more rewarding endeavors. They nest in small cavities, natural or otherwise, but do not actually excavate nest holes like woodpeckers.

BROWN CREEPER

Certhia americana

Habitat: They are equally at home in deciduous or coniferous woodlands but seem to prefer a mixture of the two.
Local Sites: City parks, river and stream bottoms, and on rare occasions patronize suet feeders, especially if peanut butter is also put out.
Status: Fairly common migrant and winter visitant. You can expect to see the first birds in the Indianapolis area during September and mid-October, with some birds remaining in choice localities throughout the winter and up till the first part of May. Rarely, birds have been noted into late May, which suggests breeding, but that has never been confirmed; they usually nest much farther north.
Length: $5^{1}/_{4}$ inches.
Remarks: The Brown Creeper is well named, as it customarily feeds by creeping around trees and picking insects out of the bark. As it

moves from one tree to another this species will begin feeding low on a tree and work its way upward in a loose spiral until it is ready to try another area. Then it will fly to the base of another tree and work its way up again. Creepers are quite unlike woodpeckers and nuthatches in appearance, having streaked brown and white backs, white under-parts, a white eyeline, and decurved bills. They appear slender for their length and are relatively long-tailed and less undulating in flight when compared to either the woodpeckers or nuthatches.

Brown Creepers have a distinctive, high-pitched call somewhat similar in quality to that of the Golden-crowned Kinglet, and indeed sometimes the two species can be found foraging together. They also occur in mixed flocks of chickadees, titmice, and Downy Woodpeckers.

CAROLINA WREN

Thryothorus ludovicianus

Habitat: Seems to prefer proximity to humans, nesting in flowerpots, cracks in garages and utility sheds, woodpecker holes, roots, crannies, and occasionally bird boxes.
Local Sites: Found in a wide variety of locations in central Indiana. The area immediately behind the nature center at Eagle Creek Park has been a good place to find at least one pair. Often they occur in suburban locations, where their ringing songs betray their presence.
Status: Common permanent residents except perhaps during severe winters, when they retreat farther south. Breed. Some years when it is exceptionally cold, as it was during 1978–79, many are apparently frozen out and the species becomes quite rare. Today they are once again common and a familiar bird about our homes.
Length: $5^1/_2$ inches.
Remarks: To paraphrase a familiar song: "Nothing could be fina than to hear a Carolina in the mor-a-ar-nin" applies very well to this sprightly inhabitant of brush piles, hedges, and small conifers in the Indianapolis area. It is a familiar bird, thanks to its engaging manner and especially its loud, rollicking, and penetrating song, which sounds like "tea-kettle tea-kettle tee-kettle." They seem to enjoy being in the vicinity of human activity, but if you approach too closely

they will chastise you with a series of harsh scolding notes. Highly inquisitive, they will investigate any unusual sound and may be enticed to show themselves. If you make a "pishing" noise, they will often perch on some exposed branch and check you out.

They use currently planted flowerpots not only for nesting but also sometimes as roosting sites—that is, places to spend the night. This has happened quite often in the Indianapolis region. The female bird generally lays from five to six whitish or pale pink eggs in a bulky nest made of a mass of leaves, twigs, hair, moss, and fine grasses. These are generally incubated for about fourteen days. Interestingly, the female is reported to remain on the nest for unusually extended periods, departing only six to seven times during the day. While she is on the nest, the male will feed her. Wrens are noted for building what are termed "dummy nests"—nests that are not used—possibly to confuse predators.

HOUSE WREN

Troglodytes aedon

Habitat: Open areas around homes, city parks, and scrubby locales. Nests in cavities and bird boxes.
Local Sites: Found in a wide variety of habitats in central Indiana ranging from urban to suburban and wooded areas.
Status: Common summer resident. Breeds. Arrives in early April and departs about mid-October.
Length: 4³/₄ inches.
Remarks: The long, sweet, bubbling song of the House Wren is its trademark. Popular with birders and non-birders alike because of its tame nature and pleasant tones, it is a familiar bird to most everyone. Because of its small size and brownish plumage, however, it is more often heard than seen, and when it is spotted it is usually hidden deep in the shrubbery, creeping from limb to limb.

They are cavity nesters, utilizing virtually any crevice to house their small nests. For years a pair nested in a neighbor's yard, the nest being placed inside an iron clothesline pole despite the close proximity of a perfectly good wren house the neighbor had installed for their use.

Wren boxes are in fact a good method of attracting these minute songsters and are simple to construct. Just remember to keep the entrance hole small, no larger than a quarter, to discourage House Sparrows. In spite of their small size, House Wrens are fearless when nesting; the decline of the Bewick's Wren in the state is attributed to this wren's habit of stealing nest sites and material from them.

House Wrens are usually solitary and are not known to flock in migration as do most other birds. They feed on a wide variety of insects and fruits, normally low to the ground. Even when singing they are seldom more than fifteen feet from the ground.

SEDGE WREN

Cistothorus platensis

Habitat: Wet grassy areas in meadows or fields.
Local Sites: The only current nesting site in the region that we know of is at Atterbury Fish and Wildlife Area in Johnson County, although they formerly nested at both Geist and Eagle Creek Reservoirs.
Status: Uncommon summer resident. Breeds. Returns to central Indiana during the first part of May with breeding taking place later in late June or early July. The fall migration begins in August and birds will continue to move southward throughout September. An occasional bird may be seen later.
Length: 4³/₄ inches.
Remarks: Among the smallest of the wrens, the Sedge Wren is also one of the most elusive. Its soft trill does not carry far and it likes to stay well hidden in the grass, making it a difficult species to locate for most of the year. Once you find it, however, the delicately colored plumage is distinctive: its white throat serves as a counterpoint to its mostly buffy underparts, well-streaked crown and back, short, slender bill, and faint buff eyestripe. In migration Sedge Wrens can be fairly common, but with the onset of the nesting season they become more difficult to find. A well-populated field where they nest one year may be completely deserted the next year for no obvious reason.

The Sedge Wren was formerly stuck with the unwieldy appellation of Short-billed Marsh Wren, an inappropriate name as they are seldom if ever found in marshlands. Their song is high pitched and insectlike with a cadence recalling a sewing machine's staccato bursts. Once you learn to recognize this call, Sedge Wrens become considerably easier to locate in the spring if you are lucky enough to find a field hosting these diminutive songbirds. They have also been heard calling at night during periods of a full moon.

RUBY-CROWNED KINGLET

Regulus calendula

Habitat: Deciduous and coniferous trees, but less apt to be found in the latter than the Golden-crowned Kinglet. Often in low brush.

Local Sites: The area near the nature center at Eagle Creek Park is a good place to see this bird during migration. Also occurs with some frequency during those seasons at University Park. Elsewhere in city parks and at suet feeders.

Status: Common migrant; arrives in early April and the last stragglers are noted in mid-May. Returns again in September until the first week of November. Occasionally found during the winter, particularly at suet feeders.

Length: 4$^{1}/_{4}$ inches.

Remarks: The Ruby-crowned Kinglet is one of the smallest birds to be seen in the Indianapolis area. The red crown patch of the male is normally hidden from view by the olive feathers of the head but can be detected occasionally when the bird becomes agitated or during courtship display. Often seen in small groups, this species is with us only during migration and rarely during the winter. Active, nervous birds, kinglets flit about in the trees and shrubbery, feeding on small insects and fruits, often in flocks of warblers and other small passerines. Despite a superficial resemblance to wood warblers they are more closely akin to our thrushes than to any other family.

Ruby-crowns are most frequently heard when scolding an owl, squirrel, or birdwatcher with a raspy, high-pitched "je-jit je-jit." Occasionally a bird will burst into a long drawn out and quite loud song—rather unusual for such a small bird. Kinglets are notorious "mobbers" and will join chickadees, titmice, and nuthatches in harassing small birds of prey and arboreal mammals whenever the opportunity presents itself. When it comes to feeding they are basically gleaners, but they do indulge in flycatching with remarkable frequency, pursuing small flying insects for short distances before returning to perch in the low branches that they normally spend their time in. They can also be seen feeding within a couple of feet of the ground in high grasses and weeds, particularly on windy days.

EASTERN BLUEBIRD

Sialia sialis

Habitat: Open areas interspersed with trees. Frequently seen perched on telephone wires and at the top of small bushes and trees. Nests in old woodpecker holes or nest boxes.

Local Sites: A bluebird trail has been established at Eagle Creek Reservoir where birds can frequently be found. Elsewhere they can occasionally be seen at Atterbury Fish and Wildlife Area and near Morgan-Monroe State Forest.

Status: Common migrant and fairly common nesting species. Spring migration usually starts early in March with birds nesting in April. Departure occurs mainly in November with some birds occurring during mild winters in the southern part of the Indianapolis area.

Length: 7 inches.

Remarks: We know of no birder or feeder watcher who does not like this beautiful species. Foreign birders who see it for the first time are amazed at the intensity of the blue on the male bird. With its back of sky blue and its delicate chestnut vest, coupled with its mild temperament, this lovely bird endears itself to everyone. It is because of this popularity that the North American Bluebird Society was formed (Box 6295, Silver Spring, MD 20906) to encourage the propagation and increase of all bluebird species.

Normally semi-permanent residents during mild winters, bluebirds sometimes perish if caught in a long spell of bad weather, especially if their food supply gets iced up. Those birds that do migrate, however, remove themselves just far enough south so that they can return early to their summer homes. This sometimes enables them to nest before their competitors, which include Tree Swallows, House Wrens, European Starlings, and House Sparrows. Bluebird trails provide them with some degree of success, and establishment of such trails in appropriate habitat is encouraged to perpetuate the species. Information about establishing one of these trails can be obtained from the above-mentioned society, and there is a chapter on bluebird trails in Lawrence Zeleny's book *The Bluebird,* available in paperback from Indiana University Press.

Although the bluebird is not what you would call an accomplished vocalist it does have a pleasant, warbling song and a distinctive call note. This call is often given in flight when the birds are moving from one area to another and is evocative of autumn, when the leaves of the trees are changing color and the first frost has covered the lower river valleys and meadows. What a tragedy it would be if it ever came to pass that the Eastern Bluebird was no longer a part of the varied birdlife of central Indiana!

VEERY

Catharus fuscescens

Habitat: Moist, dense woods with a good understory.
Local Sites: Eagle Creek Park and most city parks during migration. Also at Atterbury Fish and Wildlife Area and Morgan-Monroe State Forest.
Status: Uncommon migrant. Very rare nesting species. Migrants occur from late April to mid-May and again in September and early October.
Length: 7 inches.
Remarks: As a breeder, the Veery seems to be a relative newcomer to the Indianapolis region. Old-timers knew it as a transient, simply passing though to nesting sites farther north. They were suspected of breeding in the Indianapolis area during the early 1950s, because birds were seen during the summer at Geist Reservoir and at Fort Benjamin Harrison in the northeastern section of Marion County, but nests were never found. Young birds just out of the nest have

been located since then at Eagle Creek Park near the Scott Starling Nature Area. The nest itself is usually built on or near the ground and is constructed of twigs, weeds lined with strips of bark, and grasses. It contains from three to five pale blue eggs. Incubation usually takes from eleven to twelve days.

It has a fine song that is a favorite of many birders, evocative of the solitude of the deep wooded, moist ravines.

WOOD THRUSH

Hylocichla mustelina

Habitat: Wooded areas with little understory.
Local Sites: The area around Eagle Creek nature center and generally north of town in wooded sites. Elsewhere at Atterbury Fish and Wildlife Area and Morgan-Monroe State Forest.
Status: Fairly common summer resident. Breeds. Arrives in late April and departs in September or early October.
Length: $7^3/_4$ inches.
Remarks: Although there are some who think the Veery or Hermit Thrush has a better song, the rich, mellow, fluting song of the Wood Thrush is one of the most appealing sounds emanating from our woods in spring and certainly rivals that of any of our other summer resident species. It is a mixture of hauntingly beautiful, bell-like notes that seem to be amplified by the stillness of the deep woods. Unfortunately, they are not as common as they once were, when every wood-lot, city park, and densely forested area in Indianapolis hosted this species. The Wood Thrush is one of those indicator species that tells us if something is wrong with our environment. The loss of habitat both in Central America and in the northern part of its range (the United States and Canada) is a probable reason for the population reduction. As if this were not bad enough, the bird is heavily parasitized by the Brown-headed Cowbird. Political planners with an eye toward the future would do well to recognize that part of our legacy to succeeding generations should include the survival of such species as the Wood Thrush and establish legislation preserving mature woodlands.

The nests are a compact mass of grasses, mud, and moss, often mixed with leaf mold and paper and built anywhere from six to fifty feet above the ground in mainly deciduous trees. Here the female lays three to four pale-bluish eggs and incubates them for about thirteen days. Sometimes, in good seasons, a second nest is built after the first brood has been raised.

AMERICAN ROBIN

Turdus migratorius

Habitat: Open areas interspersed with trees near human habitation. Lawns, golf courses, and cemeteries, both urban and suburban.
Local Sites: A familiar bird around our yards and parks.
Status: Common summer and rare winter resident. Breeds. Those birds which do not winter begin returning with the spring thaws in late February when the ground becomes damp. Flocking occurs after nesting season.
Length: 10 inches.
Remarks: Traditionally considered a harbinger of spring, some robins are actually with us all winter long. They tend to be less visible in the winter, however, due to their desertion of lawns and suburbs in favor of more wooded surroundings. Then, too, they tend to flock in winter and as a result are less widespread. A common nester in suburban areas, it has little fear of human beings, often nesting over porchlights and under the eaves of houses. The nest, constructed of grass, mud, string, and small sticks, is heavily cupped in shape. Robins lay from three to six bright turquoise-blue eggs in nests that can be located as little as four feet to as high as thirty feet from the ground. At the latter height they are generally placed in the crotch formed by the branching of a limb. Two and sometimes three broods are raised each year, and it is not uncommon to see adult-sized spotted young flying and feeding in an area that also has naked nestlings being fed by adult birds.

Robins expend a great deal of energy and time pursuing their favorite prey, earthworms, about lawns and gardens in the spring and summer. The sight of a bird engaged in a life and death tug-of-war with a nightcrawler is quite comical. When the ground freezes or earthworms are in short supply, they switch to eating fruit from a number of different plants and can often be encountered feeding in mixed flocks with Cedar Waxwings. Hawthorns, the various species of honeysuckle, and Multiflora Rose are all good plants to have if you want to keep "Robin Redbreast" at your residence all year long.

Like other members of the thrush family, robins are famous for their melodious songs; their sweet refrain is a familiar sound and can be heard in the early morning hours each spring nearly everywhere.

GRAY CATBIRD

Dumetella carolinensis

Habitat: Bushes and shrubs and gardens, usually in partly open areas near forest edge.
Local Sites: City parks, suburban areas with high density of bushes and shrubs. Holliday and Eagle Creek parks, Indianapolis Museum of Art grounds are good places to find breeding birds.
Status: Common summer resident. Breeds. Arrives about the first week of May and departs in October. A few have been seen in December when they run the risk of starvation or overexposure to the elements.
Length: 8¹/₂ inches.
Remarks: The Gray Catbird is a common nesting species in the Indianapolis area. The nest itself is well concealed in extremely heavy shrubbery or brambles and is constructed of small twigs. Catbirds use habitat similar to that utilized by Brown Thrashers, and it is not uncommon to see the two species nesting side by side in the same hedgerow. They appear to be all dark gray from a distance, but up close they reveal their deep chestnut undertail coverts and a well-defined black cap. Their name derives from the distinctive, mewing call which they give when agitated; their normal vocal repertoire, however, encompasses a number of squeaky, weak calls; they are the least imitative and versatile singers of the mimid family. Catbirds have the habit of flicking their tails and wings when resting or calling in the heavy brush, a factor that aids immensely in locating them.

They are slender birds with relatively short wings, an asset in moving about in the tangles they inhabit. When disturbed, they seldom fly far, preferring instead to dive into the thickest, thorniest brambles available. Gray Catbirds feed on a wide variety of berries, seeds, and insects but appear to be especially fond of mulberries. They feed and cavort low to the ground, seldom if ever going more than twenty feet above the ground.

NORTHERN MOCKINGBIRD

Mimus polyglottos

Habitat: Dense brambles and thickets, usually near open land in agricultural areas and in the suburbs.
Local Sites: Atterbury Fish and Wildlife Area and most open areas south of Indianapolis.
Status: Common resident. Breeds. Most birds remain with us during warm winters especially in good feeding locations.
Length: 10 inches.
Remarks: One of the "mimic thrushes," mockingbirds live up to their reputation of being the premier songsters on the North American continent. One bird was heard to imitate as many as twenty-six species of birds in under an hour. Observers have related instances of mockingbirds copying their whistling and even segments of tunes heard on the radio. Even their scientific name, meaning "many-tongued imitator," reflects this habit. They are reputed to possess intelligence, cunning, and character, so much so that the Mockingbird serves as the state bird for five states. They were commonly kept as cage birds at the turn of the century and were exported to Europe in great numbers.

They seem to prefer areas with large plantings of Multiflora Rose, which they use both as a food source and for nest sites. If you wish to attract this mimic to your yard one of the best things you can plant are mulberry trees, which when fruiting host a wide variety of frugivores (fruit-eaters) including the "King of the Songsters." Mockingbirds are one of the few passerine species that will sing regularly at night, which does not endear them to residents of the suburbs who are awakened at three in the morning.

During the breeding season mockingbirds become highly territorial, vigorously defending their turf. Attacks can be vicious and other "mockers" are often attracted to join in the fray. No one is exempt, including humans, dogs, snakes, and other birds. With flashing wings, loud screeches, and spread tails, they dart in for a quick peck while another bird is distracting the intruder. In spite of their size, they still manage to discourage large egg-robbers very effectively.

It has unfairly earned a reputation for raiding gardens, but the mockingbird's diet is over one-half insects, and the fruit that is eaten is for the most part wild, not cultivated.

BROWN THRASHER

Toxostoma rufum

Habitat: Dense stands of thickets, shrubs, and bushy areas generally adjacent to open land.
Local Sites: Eagle Creek Park, most city parks, Atterbury Fish and Wildlife Area and suburban locations.
Status: Common summer resident. Breeds. Most birds arrive in mid-March and remain until about the last of October. A few birds have been seen during the winter.
Length: 11^1/$_2$ inches.
Remarks: With its rich, rusty-brown back, wings, and tail, white underparts heavily streaked with dark brown, two white wingbars, slightly decurved bill, and bright yellow eye, the Brown Thrasher is unlikely to be confused with any other species of bird in our area. It is omnivorous, feeding on a wide variety of berries, seeds, and insects.

Brown Thrashers habitually nest in the densest brambles available, although nests have been found on the ground, many yards from cover. The nest is constructed of small twigs, with the well defined central cup being lined with animal hair. Normally four eggs are laid, these being of an earthen-brown color heavily splotched with dark brown. Just prior to the nesting season is the best time to get a leisurely look at this species. At this time of year the males will sing from an exposed perch for long periods in the early morning; the song consists of a variety of phrases, with each phrase normally repeated twice, not in multiples as the Northern Mockingbird is prone to do.

CEDAR WAXWING

Bombycilla cedrorum

Habitat: Fruiting bushes and trees. Open woodland, orchards, parks, and gardens.

Local Sites: Most city parks and locally in suburban areas from time to time, especially if fruiting trees and bushes are about.

Status: Common resident but nomadic in occurrence depending on food supply. Breeds.

Length: 7¹/₄ inches.

Remarks: Gregarious frugivores (fruit-eaters) and adept flycatchers, Cedar Waxwings form large flocks in the winter and descend on fruit-bearing plants like locusts into a grain field. Flocks numbering into the hundreds are not uncommon at choice feeding locales in late winter and early spring; but, strangely enough, they are solitary nesters with rather well defined territories. They nest later than most birds in the area, usually starting in late July or early August. The nest is normally located from eight to fifteen feet off the ground in a well leaved tree, in toward the base of a branch.

Handsome birds, with black masks, beige and gray plumage, crests, yellow-tipped tails, and red wing spots, they resemble nothing so much as bandits looking for something to plunder. Their thin, reedy call is most often heard in flight, as they move from tree to tree looking for food. Rose hips, hackberries, and mulberries are among their favorite foods and are consumed in great quantities and with much gusto. In early fall they turn their attention to the flying insect hatches, flycatching from high, exposed branches or among the weeds. In winters with good crops of food, waxwings are common; in lean years they can be almost impossible to locate. Even when common they can be hard to find because they wander widely in search of food, rapidly cleaning out one supply and moving on in search of another. Few things are more beautiful than the snow-covered tree in which waxwings are feeding on brightly colored hawthorn berries or rose hips. Many are the postcards and calendars that have been produced from photographs of this species so engaged.

The Cedar Waxwing is the official emblem of our local Amos W. Butler Audubon Society.

EUROPEAN STARLING

Sturnus vulgaris

Habitat: A variety of open and lightly forested areas both urban and suburban.

Local Sites: Found readily nearly everywhere except perhaps thick woods.

Status: Common resident. Breeds. A certain portion of the population is semi-migratory.

Length: $8^1/_2$ inches.

Remarks: In our over twenty years of trapping birds for banding, the starling is certainly the smartest bird we have encountered. One of the commonest types of traps utilized for banding involves a wire cell on which a trapdoor closes behind the bird as it enters and steps on a trip pedal. Starlings are routinely able to figure out how to lift the door and escape captivity.

Originally imported to Central Park in New York City from Europe in the 1920s to help control sod webworm, this aggressive bird soon got out of control and became a problem itself. Highly competitive, they displace other birds from potential nest sites, commandeering them for their own. Their spread continentwide has been phenomenal, and they are almost certainly the commonest bird in North America today. One reason for this abundance was the building of the interstate highways, as the starlings followed along behind construction, using overpasses for nesting and roosting areas. Omnivorous and opportunistic, they do well in urban areas, feeding on refuse and food put out for more desirable species. They are actually more abundant around cities than they are in rural areas, although very few places can claim to be free of these avian rogues.

Starlings are cavity nesters, using not only old woodpecker holes and snags but drainpipes, house eaves, or any tight spot on a building that they can find and enter. This habit does not endear them to homeowners, for obvious reasons. They are also persistent. You can clean out a nest and they will have another one constructed within days in the same location. Starlings have a wide repertoire of calls, many mimicked from other species of birds. In fact, other than the Northern Mockingbird, they have the greatest variety of calls of any bird in central Indiana.

WHITE-EYED VIREO

Vireo griseus

Habitat: Dense stands of thickets, bushes, and low scrubby areas.
Local Sites: Eagle Creek Park, Atterbury Fish and Wildlife Area, and various other locations usually south of the Indianapolis region.
Status: Fairly common summer resident. Breeds. Arrives in spring in late April and departs by the first week of October.
Length: 5 inches.
Remarks: This is another of those species whose range seems to be extending farther north. Years ago it was rather rare in the Indianapolis area; today it is a fairly common summer resident. White-eyes seem to like the same type of habitat as do the Gray Catbird and Brown Thrasher, and quite often all three birds can be found together.

The nest is suspended from a twig placed two to six feet up in some small tree or bush and is composed of soft wood, bark shreds, and cobwebs and lined with fine plant down. From three to five whitish eggs decorated with a few small brown spots are laid which require from thirteen to fifteen days' incubation.

Like other members of the vireo family this species can be enticed into view by "pishing." On these occasions a small greenish-olive bird may peer at you, actually showing off its white irises, while at other times, when the bird stays hidden amid the foliage, it will sing its characteristic "per-ree-o-chick" song. To our minds that song is synonymous with the hot summer days when other birds are still except for the occasional mewing of a Gray Catbird.

YELLOW-THROATED VIREO

Vireo flavifrons

Habitat: Primarily open and mixed deciduous and coniferous forest.
Local Sites: Eagle Creek Park, Holliday Park, and the canal towpath at Butler University. Also Morgan-Monroe State Forest and the forested areas of southern Morgan County.
Status: Fairly common summer resident. Breeds. Arrives in spring about the latter part of April and departs in the fall about the last of September or first week of October.
Length: $5^1/_2$ inches.
Remarks: By the time the dog-tooth violet is in bloom in the Indianapolis area a rather harsh-sounding, slow song of two- or three-note phrases may momentarily divert your attention from the spring wildflowers to what is perhaps the most colorful member of the vireo family—the Yellow-throated Vireo. Like other members of the vireo tribe they are slow movers and once located may be studied at leisure as they feed in the upper story of the trees. Occasionally the bird may be seen to glean some insect from beneath the canopy of early emergent leaves before it moves off to the top of another nearby tree.

The breeding location of this bird, like that for so many of our small passerines, is particularly vulnerable to clear cutting of the forests, which destroys critical habitat. In particular it allows Brown-headed Cowbirds easy access to their nests and subsequent parasitism. It is highly important that such locations are protected to insure these species' survival, not only for ourselves but for future generations as well. The nest of the Yellow-throated Vireo is typically over twenty feet up, suspended in the fork of some slender tree branch, and is built primarily by the female. It is composed of moss, lichens, and fine grasses, often woven together with spider silk and plant down. In it she will lay three to five whitish eggs. Incubation is shared by both parents for some fourteen days.

Yellow-throated Vireos are persistent singers and will sometimes sing well into September. Soon after, however, the birds become quiet and move out of central Indiana to winter in Central America or northern South America.

WARBLING VIREO

Vireo gilvus

Habitat: Open forested and scrubby areas, orchards, and parks.
Local Sites: Fall Creek north of Indianapolis to Geist Reservoir, Eagle Creek, and Holliday Park, the canal towpath near Butler University, Atterbury Fish and Wildlife Area, and Morgan-Monroe State Forest.
Status: Common summer resident. Breeds. Arrives the latter part of April and departs in late September.
Length: $5^1/_2$ inches.
Remarks: There is a saying among birders: "If it's in a tree and it has totally nondescript plumage then it must be a Warbling Vireo." This is a fairly accurate assessment of the distinguishing field marks for the species—it has none. Light underneath with a dull grayish-olive back, the Warbling Vireo has a faint white line over the eye and blue-gray legs. Closest in appearance to a Tennessee Warbler and only slightly larger, it is slow moving, more heavily built, and has a heavier bill with a small hook on the tip. The song is long and warbling, more like a finch's song than that of the other vireos, and it is one of the few species in which the male will actually sing while on the nest.

The nest is built anywhere from twenty to ninety feet high in a tree, is composed of grasses, shredded leaves, and spider webs, and normally houses four offspring. Characteristically solitary, Warbling Vireos are only infrequently seen in mixed flocks of vireos and warblers and never in monospecific flocks.

RED-EYED VIREO

Vireo olivaceus

Habitat: Deciduous forested areas, second growth woodland, thickets, and gardens.
Local Sites: Eagle Creek and Holliday Parks. Morgan-Monroe State Forest and southern Morgan County.

Status: Common migrant and summer resident. Breeds. Spring birds begin appearing in late April and remain until the first week of October. There are a few records of birds remaining until November.

Length: 6 inches.

Remarks: The handsome, slow, deliberate Red-eyed Vireo is one of the characteristic birds of the forested parts of central Indiana. A very vocal bird, it frequently serenades us with its repetitious song even during the "dog days" of summer, from the tops of our tallest trees, from dawn to dusk; to our ears it seems to say: "Here I am, look at me, I see you." We have often enticed the bird to come closer by making "pishing" sounds, causing it to cock its head to one side and peer at us while seeming to wonder what manner of beast this is that makes such a strange sound. On such occasions the spectacular red iris is easily seen.

The female builds a rather deep-cupped penduline nest that is usually suspended in some horizontal fork of a tree from two to sixty feet high. Here she lays from two to four whitish eggs, sparsely marked with brownish or black dots, which take about twelve to fourteen days to hatch. Some years the species is double-brooded. Red-eyes are often heavily parasitized by Brown-headed Cowbirds and a bird will frequently be seen attempting to feed a young cowbird that is considerably larger than the parasitized parents. Later nests seem to have a better chance of surviving such parasitism.

Over the last forty years we have noticed a definite decrease in the numbers of this species and we suspect that a combination of factors is responsible—deforestation in both its summer and winter homes, increase in the numbers of Brown-headed Cowbirds, and an increase in the human population.

BLUE-WINGED WARBLER

Vermivora pinus

Habitat: Old second growth fields interspersed with trees, thickets, and brambles.

Local Sites: North end of Eagle Creek Park, Atterbury Fish and Wildlife Area. Formerly near Geist and Morse Reservoirs.

Status: Fairly common migrant and uncommon summer resident. Breeds. Arrives about the last week of April and leaves sometime in August, although fall data are lacking.

Length: 4³/₄ inches.

Remarks: One of the prettiest birds in our region, the Blue-winged Warbler is a startlingly brilliant yellow on the head and underparts, contrasting vividly with its blue-gray wings with their two white wingbars, the black eyeline, and the delicate shade of olive on the bird's back and rump. It is easily seen in May as the male sings his very distinctive high-pitched, scratchy "bee-buzz" from the top of a small tree or bush.

Although the Latin name means "pine-dwelling worm-eater," they are much more likely to be found in deciduous surroundings than in coniferous ones. The worm-eating part of the name, however, is fairly accurate, as a large percentage of their diet is composed of small caterpillars gleaned from leaves and branches. Spiders are also an important food item, and spider webs are utilized for nest building material, as are grasses garnered off the ground. The nest is usually built on the ground or within fifteen feet of it in heavy cover, as often as not surrounded by some species of brambles.

In spite of the fact that this bird hybridizes readily with the Golden-winged Warbler and that either species occasionally sings the song of the other, it has still retained its specific status. Hybrids produced are viable and are called either Brewster's or Lawrence's Warblers, depending upon whether they were sired by a Blue-winged Warbler or a Golden-winged Warbler. When these hybrids crossbreed with pure-strain birds, exact parentage becomes somewhat problematical and identification difficult.

YELLOW WARBLER

Dendroica petechia

Habitat: Second growth fields interspersed with small trees and bushes.

Local Sites: Eagle Creek Park, Atterbury Fish and Wildlife Area, and other local areas. A pair nested every year along the right-of-way of the railroad tracks at 71st Street and Highway 37 in northern Indianapolis, a highly developed part of the city.

Status: Common migrant and summer resident. Breeds. Arrives about the middle of April and departs about the first of September.
Length: 5 inches.
Remarks: One of the more noticeable sounds of spring is the short, high-pitched song of the Yellow Warbler. It is also a welcome addition to our repertoire of summer sounds. Bright yellow in color, Yellow Warblers are referred to by many non-birders as wild canaries even though they are not related to canaries at all.

Yellow Warblers nest in low bushes and trees in rather open situations and are thus a primary target for parasitism by Brown-headed Cowbirds. Cowbirds will lay their eggs in a warbler's nest and allow the warbler to raise their young. Some Yellow Warblers have learned to retaliate by abandoning the nest and building a new one. In a number of instances, they build the new nest right on top of the old one, and we have seen nests layered five stories high—an avian highrise. When on territory this little golden warrior is fearless in the defense of his domain, attacking much larger creatures with no hesitation. A beautiful bird, it is not shy and nests in suburbs and city parks, making it one of the most frequently seen warblers. In prime habitat they nest close together, almost colonially.

Although small, they are quite visible because of their constant singing, choice of open habitat, and coloration. The Latin name for this species means "tree-dweller with red-spotted skin," appropriate both from the standpoint of habitat and plumage coloration. The red spotting, however, is only found on the male, the female being a dull yellow.

YELLOW-RUMPED WARBLER

Dendroica coronata

Habitat: City parks, water courses, secondary growth, forests.
Local Sites: Easily found during migration at Eagle Creek and most city parks. In the fall, look for birds at University Park in downtown Indianapolis. A few birds can occasionally be seen in suburban areas.

Status: Common migrant, very rare in winter. One of the earliest warbler migrants, appearing in March until mid-May with returning birds spotted the latter part of September until the second week of November. Some birds tarry or remain during mild winters at choice feeding locations. They nest in the northern United States and southern Canada.

Length: 5$^1/_2$ inches.

Remarks: In spring the male birds are handsome in their black and white plumage coupled with the yellow spots on the crown of the head, at the bend of the wing, and of course—where the bird gets its name—on the rump. It was formerly called the Myrtle Warbler and so distinguished from the similar, western-occurring Audubon's Warbler until the two were found to interbreed freely where their ranges overlapped; hence the name change for both forms to "Yellow-rumped."

They are more deliberate birds than other members of the family and will often pause between feedings and allow the observer to note most of the delicacies of their plumage. In the fall, however, when their ranks are swelled by an influx of young birds, they are fairly nondescript except for the yellow rump which flashes before your eyes as the bird moves from one feeding spot to another.

Although they occasionally sing during their spring transit, more often than not their presence is betrayed by a diagnostic "check" call note that the birds persistently give as they feed in the understory of the trees. During the fall they occasionally "flycatch," launching themselves into the air trying to catch some passing insect.

CERULEAN WARBLER

Dendroica cerulea

Habitat: Usually found in the higher reaches of forested areas where it feeds and nests in the canopy.

Local Sites: At present rather restricted because of various environmental and ecological constraints. It can still be found during migration at Eagle Creek Park, Holliday Park, the Butler University towpath, and Fort Benjamin Harrison. All the former sites were at one time breeding areas. An extant breeding population occurs at Morgan-Monroe State Forest.

Status: Uncommon to rare migrant and very rare nesting species. Spring migrants arrive about the first week of May and depart in August, although the knowledge of exact departure dates is not well known.

Length: 4³/₄ inches.

Remarks: Certain species in the avian world act as biologic indicators; the Cerulean Warbler is one of them. If something happens to change our environment, such as the destruction of rain forests or temperate forest lands, then the species which inhabit those ecosystems are in jeopardy. There is some indication that this is happening with the Cerulean Warbler, for it is an inhabitant of the forest. Those who know the bird would all agree that it would be a sad day if this species disappeared from our area. Years ago it was relatively common in central Indiana, with nesting pairs located in the areas named above plus Woollen's Gardens and the now-defunct Maywood Bottoms. Except during migration, you would be hard pressed to find the bird in those areas now.

And what a bird it is! With sky-blue upper plumage and white underparts it is an attractive member of the wood warbler family, although we seldom see it well enough to note the blue dorsal plumage. Instead, we usually stare up through the surrounding canopy and note just the white undersides and perhaps the bluish necklace that encircles the throat. Although it is a small bird, it has a distinctive song which, once learned, will clinch identification—a rather burry, drawn-out "zur-zur-zur-zeee."

AMERICAN REDSTART

Setophaga ruticilla

Habitat: Found in a variety of locations like fencerows and railroad lines during migration, but generally in the more heavily forested areas of city parks and the suburbs.

Local Sites: One of the commonest species at University Park during the fall; elsewhere, look for them at Eagle Creek, Holliday, and

Marott Parks, Morgan-Monroe State Forest, and Atterbury Fish and Wildlife Area.

Status: Common migrant and uncommon summer resident. Breeds. Formerly nested at Holliday Park and Geist Reservoir and probably other wooded areas. Pairs have been seen at Eagle Creek Park and Morgan-Monroe State Forest during the summer, where they probably breed. Spring arrival is usually late April, with nesting occurring in June and departure between September and mid-October.

Length: 5¼ inches.

Remarks: An attractive member of the warbler family, the male American Redstart is a contrast of colors—deep black, flag orange, and snow white. The female is patterned like the male but the colors are muted grays and yellows with more extensive white areas on the underside. Immature fall males resemble the adult females, but the orange areas are more pronounced; immature females are largely gray with little yellow except in the tail. Flashes of orange or yellow show up like beacons as the birds cavort about on the business of survival. Residents of the forest understory, they are active birds, flitting from tree to tree in search of small insects which they collect by flycatching as well as gleaning—a study of avian perpetual motion.

OVENBIRD

Seiurus aurocapillus

Habitat: Dense understory of forested areas. During fall migration, can appear in a wider variety of habitat.

Local Sites: Forested city parks like Eagle Creek, Holliday, Marott, and Woollen's Gardens. During the fall can be found flying out of or walking among the flower plantings at University Park.

Status: Common migrant and uncommon summer resident. Breeds. Arrives in late April and departs in September or early October.

Length: 6 inches.

Remarks: Old-timers called it the Golden-crowned Warbler, but its presence would largely go undetected were it not for the loud ringing and ascending "teacher, teacher, teacher," etc., song that it gives from the undergrowth. If you look carefully you will see a rather small, thrush-like bird walking amid the leaves. It is hardly a bird that one would immediately associate with the colorful wood warbler family.

Ovenbirds construct their nests on the forest floor, usually built in a depression of dead leaves whose top is arched over with other dead leaves and vegetation. The nest itself is composed of fine grasses, plant stems, fibers, leaves, and moss, and the female constructs it on her own. From three to six whitish eggs, spotted with reddish brown, are laid and take from eleven to fourteen days to hatch. After the nesting season the birds become silent and are not easy to detect, unless stumbled upon as they feed in the dense cover so characteristic of the species.

COMMON YELLOWTHROAT

Geothlypis trichas

Habitat: Low scrubby areas with thickets, tall grasses, and small trees and shrubs.
Local Sites: Inhabits a wide variety of suburban habitat, especially the north end of Eagle Creek Park and Atterbury Fish and Wildlife Area.
Status: Common summer resident. Breeds. Arrives about mid-April and departs in October. Some birds tarry into November and even early December.
Length: 4³/₄ inches.
Remarks: Formerly called the Maryland Yellowthroat, Yellow-throated Wren, or Ground Warbler, the little Common Yellowthroat is a familiar summer resident of the Indianapolis area. It would often be overlooked were it not for its persistent, cheery song which, to many, is reminiscent of that of the Carolina Wren. It is more muted, however, and the accents are slightly different, sounding more like "witchery-witchery-witchery." Oddly enough, if you were to listen to other yellowthroats throughout their range, you would hear many different variations of that song, almost as if there were different dialects depending upon latitude and longitude; our Indianapolis bird might not even recognize its southern cousin.

They build their nests low to or on the ground in heavy vegetation, of coarse grasses, reed shreds, leaves, mosses, and other plant material. Here the female will lay from three to five whitish eggs and incubate them from eleven to thirteen days. In good years the bird will renest. Like so many of our small nesting birds this species is heavily parasitized by the Brown-headed Cowbird, and it would be quite comical, if it were not so pathetic, to see the little yellowthroat feeding a young cowbird bigger than it is.

They are inquisitive birds and can easily be brought into view by "squeaking," whereupon the bird will issue a sharp "chip" and peer at the perpetrator from amid the vegetation. At these times the black mask of the male is very noticeable, as is the bright yellow plumage. The female bird, however, being uniformly yellow, is often misidentified because it lacks the distinguishing field marks of the male bird.

YELLOW-BREASTED CHAT

Icteria virens

Habitat: Scrubby open areas interspersed with thickets, small trees, and bushes.

Local Sites: Atterbury Fish and Wildlife Area, the north end of Eagle Creek Park, and formerly Geist and Morse Reservoirs.

Status: Fairly common summer resident. Breeds. Spring arrival is during the latter part of April. Fall departure is not well documented but is believed to occur mainly in August and September, with an occasional bird remaining into October.

Length: 7½ inches.

Remarks: The Yellow-breasted Chat is an anomaly in the warbler family, for it looks and acts more like a member of the mimid family (mockingbirds, etc.) than a warbler. To some extent it even sounds more like that family too. A denizen of the thick brush, thorny bushes, and undergrowth, the chat is more often heard than seen, as it seems to delight in a spasm of song. Those lucky enough to observe one undetected will notice that the bird goes through a series of contortions and aerial gyrations in accompaniment to its vocalizations.

This bird, our largest warbler, builds a nest constructed of leaves, vines, and grasses about two to six feet off the ground in some bush or briar tangle. Here the female lays from three to six white, brown-speckled eggs, with incubation taking about eleven days. In banding studies south of town we repeatedly retrapped a chat for several years in succession, proving that this particular bird returned to the same area each year.

SCARLET TANAGER

Piranga olivacea

Habitat: Mature deciduous forests and woodland.
Local Sites: Eagle Creek Park, Holliday Park, Woollen's Gardens, and Morgan-Monroe State Forest. In migration appears in a wider variety of habitat from city parks to the suburbs.
Status: Common migrant and rare summer resident. Breeds. Arrives about the last week of April and remains until late September or early October.
Length: 7 inches.
Remarks: This dazzling gem is one of four highly colorful species belonging to the tanager family in North America. Of the four, two are rare summer residents in central Indiana—the Summer Tanager and the more common Scarlet Tanager. Brilliant scarlet with black wings, the male is surely one of our most beautiful woodland birds, much sought after by beginning birders and seasoned veterans alike. Females are a dull yellowish-olive, an adaptation which helps camouflage them on the nest. In spite of the male's bright colors he can at times be difficult to locate in the forest canopy, even when he sings. His song has been described as robin-like, but it is slightly slower and has a burry or scratchy quality that is different from the clear, ringing tones of the robin. With the coming of fall the male gradually molts into a plumage similar to that of the female before the species begins its exodus to South America for the winter months.

Tanagers are omnivorous, feeding on insects and wild fruit such as fox grapes, elderberries, and mulberries. They will occasionally come to feeding stations if given offerings of oranges, bananas, or other fruit. Tanagers are really neotropical birds. In the Neotropics, that portion of the Western Hemisphere between the Tropics of Cancer and Capricorn, over one hundred species of tanagers can be found in a wide variety of habitats.

NORTHERN CARDINAL
Cardinalis cardinalis

Habitat: Found nearly everywhere, from city parks and backyards to forest edges.
Local Sites: City parks, both suburban and urban locations. Easily enticed to feeding stations with oil sunflower seed.
Status: Common permanent resident. Breeds.
Length: 8³/₄ inches.
Remarks: Known to many as the Redbird, the Northern Cardinal is welcome at any birdwatcher's feeder. Because it is beautiful and has a cheery song, seven states—Indiana, Illinois, North Carolina, Kentucky, Ohio, Virginia, and West Virginia—have declared it their official state bird, more than any other species, and many Audubon groups, including the Indiana Audubon Society, have adopted the cardinal as their symbol. And of course several professional sports teams use the cardinal for their mascot, including the Saint Louis Cardinals, the Phoenix Cardinals, and the Louisville Redbirds. This species is especially vocal, with male birds singing from dawn to dusk from late February until August. They are frequent visitors to feeders containing oil sunflower seeds—an especially good attractant. Be sure to keep a good supply on hand, as they are hearty eaters.

Cardinals are the bane of bird banders and researchers, biting viciously when handled and squirming violently in an effort to escape. It is difficult to decide which is prettier, the male or female; the male is bright red all over with some black about the bill, while the female is a mixture of beige, gray, and red. Both sexes have a crest, which gives them a pert, attentive look. Cardinals are the largest members of the finch family found in central Indiana with any regularity. Somewhat migratory, there are more birds present in winter when the local populations are augmented by birds from farther north. They are especially noticeable at this season due to the lack of vegetation and their presence at feeding stations. They nest in low shrubbery along wooded edges and in suburbs and are subject to parasitism by Brown-headed Cowbirds.

ROSE-BREASTED GROSBEAK
Pheucticus ludovicianus

Habitat: Deciduous forest and woodlands. In migration found in a wider variety of habitats from scrub to forest.
Local Sites: City parks, Atterbury Fish and Wildlife Area, Woollen's Gardens, Holliday and Marott Parks, and wooded areas during migration. A pair nested at Eagle Creek Park some years ago.
Status: Common migrant and very rare summer resident. Breeds. Arrives in late April and breeds in late May or early June. The fall migration lasts from September until the last week of October, with some birds tarrying into early November.
Length: 8 inches.
Remarks: The male Rose-breasted Grosbeak is certainly one of the most beautiful denizens of central Indiana with its dazzling coat of black and white coupled with the brilliant red patch on its throat and reddish marks under the wings. We have even had telephone calls about black and white birds that were apparently bleeding from the chest, so vivid is the color of red on the bird. It is also a pleasant singer, sounding quite like the muted song of the American Robin but less harsh. Nests are typically built in the fork of some tree, usually from six to twenty-six feet high, and are so loosely constructed that the eggs often show through from underneath. The female lays from three to six spotted, pale greenish-blue eggs which generally take from twelve to fourteen days to hatch. Unfortunately, this is another species that is heavily parasitized by the Brown-headed Cowbird, for its nests are easy for that species to find.

INDIGO BUNTING
Passerina cyanea

Habitat: Open areas of forests or forest edgings with extensive undergrowth of shrubs, thickets and agricultural areas.

Local Sites: City parks, especially Eagle Creek, Starkey, Holliday. Also found at Atterbury Fish and Wildlife Area, Geist and Morse Reservoirs, agricultural areas in central Indiana.

Status: Common summer resident. Breeds. Birds return in late April and depart in early October. On rare occasions a bird will try to overwinter in our region, almost always with disastrous results.

Length: 5¹/₂ inches.

Remarks: A little bit of electric-blue sky, the Indigo Bunting is mistakenly called the "bluebird" by many non-birders. Its startling shades of deep, iridescent blue make it one of the most colorful and noticeable birds of the forest edge. Only the male displays this scintillating color; the female is of a plain, earthen-brown tone with few outstanding characteristics. Males are visible all summer long as they sing their clear, sweet song from exposed fences, telephone wires, or dead branches from dawn to dusk. As winter approaches, buntings begin to flock for their southward migration, at which point the males begin to molt out of their bright nuptial plumage to assume the less conspicuous shades of the female.

Buntings belong to the finch family, whose members are characterized by their short, heavy, conical bills. This particular bill shape is an adaptation for feeding on seeds, many of which need to be removed from husks or shells before consumption. Indigo Buntings are small birds, but are both common enough and beautiful enough to make an obvious presence on any bird outing. They call attention to themselves when not singing by uttering a sharp "chip" when taking flight or skirmishing over their territories.

Indigo Buntings nest low to the ground, within five feet, in very heavy cover. Nests are built from a variety of grasses and plant materials. They are only about four inches in diameter, deeply cupped, and hold three to five eggs.

RUFOUS-SIDED TOWHEE

Pipilo erythrophthalmus

Habitat: Dense patches of briars, thickets, and scrubby open areas.

Local Sites: Scrubby suburban areas and particularly Eagle Creek Park and Atterbury Fish and Wildlife Area. Occasionally comes to feeding stations, especially in the winter.

Status: Common summer resident. Breeds. Birds normally return in late March and leave in November or early December. Very rare in winter.

Length: $8^1/_2$ inches.

Remarks: Not easily confused with any other bird, the males of this species look quite elegant with their rufous sides and vent, black head, chin, throat, back, wings, and tail, their white breast and belly, and a dash of white on tail and wings. This contrasting plumage is accented by a bright red eye which seems to glow with an internal fire all its own. Females are similar to the males but all the black is replaced by a rich brown. Rarely, a bird of the western subspecies known as the Spotted Towhee will show up in Indiana; these individuals have pronounced white spots covering their backs and are readily distinguishable from local birds.

Towhees spend a large amount of their time scratching about on the ground in heavy undergrowth looking for insects and seeds to feed upon. They create a great deal of noise as they hop among the dry leaves and grass, thus attracting attention to themselves. The males' full song has been described as "drink-your-tea" but more often than not they simply call "treeee" or a short "chwink." A ground-loving species, they are usually encountered low down in heavy scrub and when flushed fly low along the ground to another thicket.

Normally seen singly, or at best in pairs, Rufous-sided Towhees often associate with other members of the sparrow family in overgrown fields and fencerows.

AMERICAN TREE SPARROW

Spizella arborea

Habitat: Overgrown fields, agricultural areas, and scrubby areas.

Local Sites: North end of Eagle Creek Park. Geist and Morse Reservoirs, Atterbury Fish and Wildlife Area, and overgrown fields in agricultural areas.

Status: Common winter visitant, appearing around Thanksgiving and leaving in late March or early April.

Length: 6¹/₄ inches.

Remarks: With its subtle colors the American Tree Sparrow is one of our prettier sparrows and does much to dispel the myth that sparrows are little drab, brown birds that all look alike. Sporting a perky rusty cap, eyeline, whisker mark, and wingbar offset with white, this species shows color with restraint. A clear breast with one central dark spot separates the American Tree Sparrow from the other two rusty-capped species in Indiana, the Chipping and Field Sparrows.

During a typical winter they sometimes intermingle with other species such as Common Redpolls, American Goldfinches, and Field Sparrows but are more often seen in large homogeneous flocks, moving from one feeding area to the next. At these times they keep up a continuous and pleasing call which has been likened to the sound of icicles tinkling in the wind; to us, it connotes those wild semi-arctic areas where the species breeds.

CHIPPING SPARROW

Spizella passerina

Habitat: Found in city parks and well-manicured lawns and gardens in the suburbs.

Local Sites: Eagle Creek Park, Holliday Park, Butler University campus and canal towpath. Elsewhere a familiar bird in most of our suburbs.

Status: Common summer resident. Breeds. Arrives in early April and remains until late October. We know of no valid winter records. Winter records attributed to this species are more likely to be of the American Tree Sparrow.

Length: 5¹/₂ inches.

Remarks: The trim and slender Chipping Sparrow is a familiar sight around suburban homes and gardens, since it seems to feel more at ease around humans than around members of its own family. The Chippy resembles the American Tree Sparrow but lacks that species' black breast dot. Our records indicate that the Chippy is not as common as it was some forty years ago, perhaps due to some change in lawn care involving indiscriminate use of pesticides or lawn care products.

Chipping Sparrows build their nests in small trees, usually conifers, or sometimes shrubs or vines, anywhere from one to twenty-five feet from the ground. The nest is constructed of fine grasses and weed stalks, often lined with hair, and the four bluish-green eggs usually take from eleven to fourteen days to hatch. In good years the species is double brooded.

Adult birds sport a chestnut cap and a sharp white line over the eye during the spring. Young birds and fall plumaged adult birds tend to have more of a striped cap, often causing birding neophytes to mistake them for the much rarer Clay-colored Sparrow. Toward fall, small groups can be found feeding in gravel driveways or along roadways gleaning seeds from the mature grass. The song from which it derives its name is usually given from atop a house or small tree and is a rather monotonous, rapid chipping trill.

FIELD SPARROW

Spizella pusilla

Habitat: Old field edges and rather open areas interspersed with small trees or bushes.

Local Sites: A familiar bird in suburban old fields and at Eagle Creek Park, Atterbury Fish and Wildlife Area, and Walnut Grove. Often found in cultivated areas where there are extensive fencerows undisturbed by cutting.

Status: Common summer resident. Breeds. Appears in late March and remains until November. Some mild winters a few birds may be found in choice habitat.

Length: 5³/₄ inches.

Remarks: One of the commoner species of sparrow in its chosen habitat of brushy fields; in the spring, summer, and fall it can easily be located by its characteristic song, which sounds like a ping-pong ball dropping on a tile floor. Males sing from an exposed perch such as the top of a tall weed, hedge, or low-slung limb and are then readily spotted. This is one of the few birds that will occasionally sing in the evening when there is a full moon. Field Sparrows are a ground nesting species, laying four to six eggs in a well-developed cup of woven grasses and horsehair hidden deep in a dense clump of grass or weeds. The eggs are small and are heavily spotted with dark brown or a tan background. Fledged young are similar in appearance to adults but exhibit substantial streaking on the breast and flanks.

It is a small bird with two distinct wingbars, a pink bill and legs, and a rusty cap, and is not often confused with other members of the sparrow family. Sparrows in general are often thought of as drab, unappealing creatures, but the subtle coloration of this little grass-lander is attractive even to the most jaded eye. Field Sparrows are normally seen foraging close to the ground as they flit from bush to bush in search of the insects and weed seeds upon which they feed.

SONG SPARROW

Melospiza melodia

Habitat: Open scrubby fields, suburban lawns interspersed with bushes, thickets and brambles.
Local Sites: A familiar bird of the suburbs and city parks.
Status: Common permanent resident. Breeds. In winter the local population is augmented by more northerly migratory birds.
Length: 6¼ inches.
Remarks: This little bird more than makes up for its drabness with a delightful song. Although it is usually given in all its glory at the height of the breeding season, when male birds ascend to some favorite perch, a more muted version may be heard during the late winter, when most other birds are relatively silent. At that time of the year it seems to foretell better days ahead.

The Song Sparrow is one of those little brown birds that are difficult to see unless they are perched upon some singing post or enticed into the open with "pishing" noises, at which time the observer may get a clearer view of the breast streaking, noting that it tends to terminate further down on the breast in a more or less well defined spot.

Song Sparrows' nests are well hidden on the ground under a tuft of grass or in a small bush, rarely as high as twelve feet. The three to five greenish-blue eggs are blotched with reddish-brown or purplish spots and hatch in twelve to thirteen days. This species is heavily parasitized by the Brown-headed Cowbird and it is quite common to see the little Song Sparrow feeding a fledgling cowbird. Fortunately, most birds will renest at least once more in a good year, with the second nesting better timed to avoid interlopers.

It is strictly a ground feeder. Those wishing to attract the bird to their feeding stations should spread a thin scattering of corn and seeds on the ground. They often inhabit overgrown city lots abandoned to weeds, where they can forage and establish territories. This habit led to the award-winning life history study done near Columbus, Ohio, by a housewife named Margaret Nice—proof that all of us can contribute some new and interesting knowledge concerning our birdlife.

WHITE-THROATED SPARROW

Zonotrichia albicollis

Habitat: Scrubby undergrowth of tangles and brambles, often with other species of sparrows. Frequently seen in the suburbs at feeding stations.

Local Sites: The feeding station at the Indianapolis Museum of Art is a good place to view this species in winter. During migration it occurs in a wide variety of sites, notably Eagle Creek, Holliday, Marott, and Starkey Parks, and Atterbury Fish and Wildlife Area. The canal towpath near Butler University is also a likely spot.

Status: Common migrant, occurring most frequently in April to mid-May and then again from early October to early December. A few birds will winter in choice feeding areas.

Length: 6³/₄ inches.

Remarks: White-throated Sparrows are ground feeders; they forage for seeds, berries, and insects by hopping about and scratching through the fallen leaves. Adults are distinctive, with their white striped heads, yellow lores, double wingbars, and well-defined white throats. Young birds are harder to identify, but still have the well-defined white throat and dark bill of the adult along with a well-streaked breast and the characteristic hunched posture of the species.

This is one of the larger sparrows, a considerable proportion of which is tail. They are a flocking species; in winter it is not unusual to see several moving through the underbrush. Often other sparrows, primarily White-crowned and Song Sparrows, intermingle with these congregations to feed. They are frequent visitors to feeding stations in suburban and rural areas, eating millet, sunflower seed, and cracked corn. In the spring their familiar song can be heard just about anywhere, a clear whistle that has been likened to "Old Sam Peabody, Peabody, Peabody." Unlike many male sparrows, the White-throated sings from deep within cover rather than from an exposed perch.

WHITE-CROWNED SPARROW

Zonotrichia leucophrys

Habitat: Scrubby areas of thickets and brambles, especially near old open fields. They particularly like to winter in locations with good stands of Multiflora Rose. Railroad rights-of-way.
Local Sites: Atterbury Fish and Wildlife Area, Eagle Creek Park, and suburban areas with good stands of Multiflora Rose.
Status: Common migrant and winter visitor, arriving in late October and staying until about the second week of May. They nest far to the north of us, in Canada.
Length: 7 inches.
Remarks: The adult White-crowned Sparrow is a handsome bird with a boldly striped crown of white and black, a pink bill, and a gray throat. At least two subspecies have been seen in the Indianapolis region, the common one having black lores and the other having white lores, which indicates a bird of a more western distribution. Immature birds are similar to the adults, but the black and white head striping is replaced by brown and tan lines.

This is a flocking species, and is generally found in groups of twenty to thirty, although at times we have seen even larger flocks. Frequently they can also be found in the company of other sparrow species, primarily White-throated Sparrows, as they move about the brush. Multiflora Rose is one of their favorite types of cover, and they can be approached rather closely when they feel safely hidden in the thorn-laden branches of a row of brambles. They are consistent visitors to feeding stations, eating millet, cracked corn, and sunflower seeds. In the fall and spring when insects are active they will take numbers of arthropods such as grasshoppers and beetles to supplement their diet.

On mild winter days and in early spring their clear, sweet song can be heard ringing out as they begin selecting mates for the summer months in preparation for raising future generations.

DARK-EYED JUNCO

Junco hyemalis

Habitat: Open fields interspersed with small bushes, city parks, and suburban areas.
Local Sites: A familiar wintering species found in a wide variety of sites, from city parks to the suburbs.
Status: Common winter visitor, appearing in late September and remaining until mid-April. A few birds are seen in early May.
Length: 6¹/₄ inches.
Remarks: How dull winter would be without this little sparrow or snowbird, as it is sometimes called. Primarily a ground feeder, it cheers us with its calm demeanor and its attractive if somewhat somber plumage. They are easy to identify. It has been aptly written that their backs are the color of the leaden sky, while their white underparts resemble the snow on the ground. Juncos travel about in small flocks, sometimes in the company of American Tree Sparrows, and make regular visits to feeding stations where they feed almost exclusively on the ground. They especially like cracked corn but will feed nearly as well on millet and oil sunflower seeds. By planting low shrubs nearby you can offer the birds some protection from potential predators and the elements.

Juncos are normally rather quiet, occasionally uttering a few simple chips while traveling to and from the feeding areas. Toward spring, however, an occasional bird will break into a rather long drawn-out, chipping song reminiscent of that of the Chipping Sparrow. As winter progresses, a definite change can be noted in the restless activity of the feeding birds: they become more intolerant of one another, with frequent skirmishes, mock battles, and much chasing. At this time their white outer tail feathers become most conspicuous as they flash them by alternately closing and unclosing the grayish inner feathers. One day in April they are here and the next day, all of a sudden, they disappear, not to return to us until next October.

BOBOLINK

Dolichonyx oryzivorus

Habitat: Grassy fields and wet meadows, prairie, and among cultivated grains, alfalfa, and clover.
Local Sites: Atterbury Fish and Wildlife Area, where they nest. During migration, look for them in newly emergent hayfields and grassy meadows, especially in Boone and Shelby Counties.
Status: Fairly common migrant and uncommon summer resident. Breeds. Arrives about the last week of April and departs in early September.
Length: 7 inches.
Remarks: The migratory patterns of the Bobolink are a marvel of nature. It nests in many of the eastern states north of the Ohio River into the prairie regions of Canada and travels to its winter home, northern Argentina, after the breeding season—one of the longest migrations for a land bird.

Returning male birds are among the most beautiful of the songbirds with their black and white plumage set off by a patch of buffy yellow on the back of the head. When they arrive in spring the male birds set up territories and perform an exuberant courtship flight, hovering above the tall grass, sometimes mounting high in the sky and returning earthward, all the while emitting a cheerful, bubbling song that is unforgettable. They seem to delight in their existence.

Finding a Bobolink's nest is a matter of pure luck, for they hide them very well in dense cover. It is constructed of weed stalks and grasses and is generally built in a small scrape in the ground with four to seven grayish-buff eggs, splotched with brown. Incubation takes about thirteen days. Young birds are miniature editions of the adult female, with muted sparrow-like streakings of black, brown, and orange buff.

In August the male birds begin to molt into their more nondescript winter plumage and gather with the females and young of the year into small flocks prior to their departure for South America.

RED-WINGED BLACKBIRD

Agelaius phoeniceus

Habitat: Wet marshes, fens, lake and river borders, and open fields, either agricultural or non-agricultural.
Local Sites: A familiar bird nearly everywhere except in urban habitat.
Status: Common summer resident. Breeds. Although a few may winter, the majority move out of the area. The male birds return during the first warm days of February with the females following a week or two later. They remain until cold weather moves them out in late November or early December.
Length: 8³/₄ inches.
Remarks: The Red-winged Blackbird is a highly vocal and visible species, observable to even the novice birdwatcher. In our area there seem to be two distinct populations, those that nest in cattail marshes and those that prefer overgrown weedy fields or agricultural areas. The latter population seems to be a fairly recent adaptation to modern agricultural practices. Their omnivorous and opportunistic habits often lead to conflicts with grain farmers because the birds may go in after planting and strip a field of all the seed; but, as if in an act of contrition, they also perform the valuable service of eating large numbers of insects that are harmful to crops. During the winter months they form huge roosts with other species of blackbirds and starlings, sometimes numbering into the millions, and can be quite disruptive with their constant calling and the deposition of large quantities of guano in residential areas. These enormous flocks also present a haz-

ard when located near airports, as low-flying aircraft suck them into turbines or prop blades.

Nests are built out of weeds or cattails, depending upon the habitat preferred, but are invariably located within three feet of the ground and sometimes on the ground itself. Four to six eggs are laid but it is seldom that all hatch; predators such as snakes, raccoons, and skunks find the nest easy to locate and often reach the progeny before they fledge and can reach safety. This is somewhat offset by the Red-wing's tendency to nest in loose colonies, ensuring the survival of at least some young. Another breeding strategy adopted by the species is to raise multiple broods each summer.

Male Red-winged Blackbirds are handsome birds with their glossy black plumage and their red and yellow shoulder patches, a feature much in evidence during the courtship season. Females are heavily streaked and bear a resemblance to oversized sparrows except for the light red wash on their throat and breast.

EASTERN MEADOWLARK

Sturnella magna

Habitat: Open fields and meadows.
Local Sites: Atterbury Fish and Wildlife Area, Indianapolis International Airport, and some agricultural areas around the region.
Status: Common summer resident. Breeds. Very rare in winter depending upon food supply. Early migrants appear in March and remain until about the first week of December.
Length: 9¹/₂ inches.
Remarks: In no way related to the larks, the Eastern Meadowlark is in fact a member of the blackbird family. Its overall build is similar to that of the European Starling, but meadowlarks are notable for their bright yellow throat and breast, interrupted by a broad black "V" on the upper chest. They sport a boldly striped crown of dark brown and white, have a streaked brown back, and show white outer tail feathers in flight. Generally they are most easily seen while singing their clear whistled song of "see-you, see-year" from fence posts or wires.

They resemble a small quail when rustling about in the grass in search of food. Their diet consists of a wide variety of insects, seeds, and berries, most of which is gathered off the ground. Meadowlarks nest on the ground in dense clumps of grass. The nest is a medium-sized cup of woven grass and is very difficult to locate, as the female lands some distance from the nest and approaches it from the ground. Young meadowlarks are out of the nest and active sometime in late June or early July but are seldom seen due to their excellent camouflage and habit of "freezing" when perceived danger is nearby.

COMMON GRACKLE

Quiscalus quiscula

Habitat: Partly open areas, usually around human habitation, nesting in either coniferous or deciduous trees.

Local Sites: Easy to see in both urban and suburban areas.

Status: Common summer resident, very rare during the winter. First migrants often appear in mixed flocks of other icterids in late February. Most depart in late November or early December. Sizable fall roosts, numbering from several hundred to several thousand occur, in September and October along White River south of Indianapolis.

Length: $12^1/_2$ inches.

Remarks: Aside from the European Starling and the House Sparrow few birds are held in such contempt as the Common Grackle. With its large size and aggressive behavior it is the terror of feeding stations, chasing more desirable birds away and creating a mess by swiping its bill back and forth in the feed, scattering grain hither and yon. If you feed birds, you must resign yourself to hosting this ruffian.

Fall roosts, which are generally sizable, often contain a congregation of other species like the Red-winged Blackbird, Brown-headed Cowbird, and European Starling. In residential areas, the constant din these flocks create as they arrive and depart and the resultant unhealthy conditions are of some concern. In southern states, where these congregations can be quite bothersome, the spraying of such areas with detergents, which dissolve the oily protection on the birds' feathers, or the use of noise (produced by firing carbide cannons) generally disperses the birds.

In the spring, male birds court the females through pursuit and by an elaborate ground display, puffing up their chest feathers as if to better show off their iridescence, to the accompaniment of grating, harsh calls reminiscent of the opening and closing of a rusty gate. After courtship they usually nest in trees, in colonies of from twenty to thirty pairs, as high as sixty feet above the ground. Here the female lays three to six pale-greenish eggs and incubates them about eleven or twelve days.

Although not a very appealing bird it seems safe to say that the Common Grackle is one of those highly adaptable species that is destined to remain part of our avifauna for some time.

BROWN-HEADED COWBIRD

Molothrus ater

Habitat: Forested areas, particularly forest edge, parks, gardens, and feeding stations.

Local Sites: A familiar bird in the suburbs, utilizing gardens and park areas as well as forests. In the last twenty years it has been patronizing feeding stations in the winter, and can sometimes be a pest.

Status: Common summer resident. Breeds. At times very common in the winter at feeding stations. Forms roosts with other blackbird species. Those birds which migrate tend to return in late February and leave in November.

Length: $7^1/_2$ inches.

Remarks: Cowbirds take the prize for being the worst parents in the bird world! Parasitic, they lay their eggs in other birds' nests, leaving them to be hatched and raised by foster parents. Young cowbirds grow more rapidly and are usually larger than the host species' young, and all too often push them out of the nest or commandeer all of the incoming food. But this tactic is not always successful. Some species have learned to recognize cowbird eggs and summarily eject them from the nest. One species, the Yellow Warbler, actually constructs a new nest, frequently over the top of the old nest and the invading egg.

Because of their parasitic habits cowbirds present a danger to several species of rare birds. In northern Michigan and central Texas, where the Kirtland's Warbler and the Black-capped Vireo, respectively, nest, cowbirds are sometimes trapped to give the desirable species a greater chance of reproductive success. These trapped birds are in some instances relocated and in others destroyed.

The cowbird is a polyandrous species, meaning the females mate with several males during the breeding season, an unusual situation in the avian community. In April it is not uncommon to see a female surrounded by several strutting, calling males.

Cowbirds can become nuisances at bird feeders in the winter, arriving in large flocks and consuming all of the seed placed out for songbirds. Forming huge flocks in the winter, they are a major farm pest and prove inconvenient in suburbs because of the noise and subsequent filth that they generate. Their short, heavy beaks and their distinctive profile can be a reliable field mark in low or obscure lighting.

ORCHARD ORIOLE

Icterus spurius

Habitat: Old field and orchard areas interspersed with trees in the thirty foot range.

Local Sites: Atterbury Fish and Wildlife Area and north end of Eagle Creek Park.

Status: Fairly common summer resident. Breeds. Arrives in early May and departs the latter part of August or first part of September.

Length: 7¼ inches.

Remarks: The Orchard Oriole is slightly smaller and much more slender than the Northern Oriole, its better-known cousin. Male Orchards are subdued-looking birds for orioles; the head, throat, back, wings, and tail are black; the rump, belly, vent, and epaulets are a deep ocher color. Old-timers used to call them Bastard Orioles because this subdued coloration mimics the bright orange of the Northern. Females are a bright yellow-green below, unlike the yellow-orange of the female Northern Orioles. As with most orioles, it takes two years for the male to acquire his adult colors. First year males are similar to females but have a well-defined black bib on their throat and chest as well as a darker back.

The nest is constructed of woven grasses placed in the fork of a limb and lacks the pendulous quality of the Northern Oriole's nest. First year males are usually present at nest sites and help in the feeding and care of the newly hatched young. You can occasionally entice them to feeders by putting out grapes, apples, or oranges, but they are not consistent feeder visitors, preferring instead to forage for wild food.

The song of the Orchard Oriole is very different from that of the Northern, being longer, more melodic, and warbling, sounding somewhat like a finch.

NORTHERN ORIOLE

Icterus galbula

Habitat: Open woodland and forest edge, orchards, city parks, and some suburban areas.
Local Sites: Atterbury Fish and Wildlife Area, Eagle Creek Park, the canal towpath near Butler University, Fall Creek north to Geist Reservoir, and some suburban areas.
Status: Common summer resident. Breeds. Arrives about the last week of April and departs in September.
Length: 8³/₄ inches.
Remarks: It is hard to believe that these gorgeous birds are in the same family as the blackbirds. With their bright orange, black, and white feathers, they resemble tanagers rather than icterids, but their slim body structure and calls are more akin to true blackbirds than to any other group. This species constructs an unusual penduline nest, hanging as much as two feet below a branch rather than resting on it, with the entrance located on the side of the nest several inches up from the bottom. This peculiar arrangement makes it difficult for predators to gain entrance to the eggs and young. Arboreal in nature, Northern Orioles nest twenty or more feet off the ground and do most of their foraging in the canopy. We once saw a pair attempt to collect a long piece of kite string that had been draped across a tele-

phone wire and into a conifer tree. Both birds kept tugging on the end of the string, trying their best to extricate it in order to incorporate it into their nest. They were unsuccessful until one of us cut the string into smaller, more manageable pieces. The nest is usually made of woven grasses, vines, and spider webs, and because of its construction has a tendency to sway in even the slightest breeze.

Primarily nocturnal migrants, flocks of these birds can sometimes be seen on early spring mornings flying low over the treetops on their way north. In many cases young birds from the previous year's nesting will return and assist the adults in raising their new batch of young, helping out by bringing food to the young and removing waste materials from the nest. These first year birds resemble the adults but are duller in color and have more restricted areas of black on the head.

Originally named the Baltimore Oriole, this species has been "lumped" with the Bullock's Oriole, a western counterpart, to create the Northern Oriole. The two subspecies interbreed extensively in their zone of overlap, and viable hybrids are common.

HOUSE FINCH

Carpodacus mexicanus

Habitat: Urban and suburban areas interspersed with conifers and deciduous trees. Also agricultural areas and city parks.

Local Sites: A familiar feeder visitor in the Indianapolis region, and found in a wide variety of habitats.

Status: Common resident. Breeds. In winter, roving flocks, some from other areas, visit bird feeders where they compete with other species.

Length: 6 inches.

Remarks: On Saturday, 28 March 1976, we observed a strange finch as it came to the feeders at the Horticultural Center at the Indianapolis Museum of Art. Superficially resembling a Purple Finch, it fed with a mixed flock of American Goldfinches and other species. We determined that it was a male House Finch and tried unsuccessfully to capture it using mist nets. Later we talked to a local photographer,

Tom Field, and learned that he had photographed the bird several days previously under the impression that it was an aberrant Purple Finch. That photograph established the first physical proof of the occurrence of the House Finch in Indiana.

Why had this western bird come to be there? Apparently, sometime in the 1940s, alert Fish and Wildlife agents found that several New York bird dealers were selling this species under the name of Hollywood Finches and ordered their subsequent release. From that original release the bird has spread westward, appearing and nesting in most states between New York and the Mississippi River. It has now become one of the most common birds in central Indiana and is locally abundant.

The nest is a rather messy affair of loosely constructed twigs, grasses, and debris placed in tree cavities, bird boxes, building ledges, and conifers. Like the Northern Cardinal, the male bird feeds the female prior to and after courtship.

The male bird is a handsome fellow with a reddish face, bib, and rump, while the female looks sparrow-like, with brown streaks and overall somber plumage.

Interestingly, the bird seems to compete with the equally abundant House Sparrow. Dr. Charles D. Wise of Ball State University has documented several instances indicative of this competition. Who knows, maybe the House Finch will soon displace that noxious species as one of the most undesirable visitors to bird feeders. In any event, the sight of a few dozen male House Finches at the thistle feeder in mid-January is a welcome sight and helps alleviate those winter spells of "cabin fever."

RED CROSSBILL

Loxia curvirostra

Habitat: Coniferous or mixed deciduous-coniferous forests.
Local Sites: Eagle Creek Park is the best place to see this species during flight years. It has been known to visit bird feeders occasionally.

Status: An erratic winter visitor occurring during flight or "finch" years from November into December, rarely later.

Length: 6¹/₂ inches.

Remarks: The Red Crossbill is one of the birds termed "erratic winter finches," appearing some years while completely absent for many years. Apparently their occurrence is tied in with the availability of a winter food supply farther north, affecting whether we see them in the Indianapolis area or not. Back in the 1950s a local birding stir was created when a small group of these birds were located during late December at the Eagle Creek Forest Preserve (forerunner to Eagle Creek Park) by a group of young birdwatchers. That particular flock of birds remained until well into May of the following year.

The bird gets its name from the fact that the bill is indeed crossed, a characteristic that improves its food-gathering power by enabling it to crack open and extract seeds from pine cones. According to some old-time descriptions of the bird, the crossed bill was the result of its attempts to extract the nails from Jesus' cross on Calvary nearly two thousand years ago.

Male birds are a muted rose-red color while the female is a subdued greenish-olive. When feeding or flying from one area to another the birds often emit a characteristic and far-carrying call note. This, one would think, would normally be very helpful in locating the birds except that it is also ventriloquial in nature and just as easily could lure the seeker off in another direction.

During those rare years when crossbills occur here, they are a welcome addition and one that only stimulates our interest in the mystery of nature.

PINE SISKIN

Carduelis pinus

Habitat: Coniferous and mixed coniferous-deciduous forested areas.

Local Sites: During finch years, found readily at suburban feeders or at the Horticultural Center at the Indianapolis Museum of Art, and also at Eagle Creek Park, where it seems to prefer feeding in sweet gum trees. At these times it can often be seen side by side with the American Goldfinch.

Status: Erratic rare to common winter visitor and very rare summer resident. Breeds. Most non-nesting birds occur between late September until the first week of May.

Length: 5 inches.

Remarks: One of the "winter finches" and sometimes a very common winter visitor, the Pine Siskin can at other times be difficult to locate due to its cyclical wandering patterns. In optimal years they begin arriving in late September and mix with American Goldfinches to form flocks of anywhere from a couple of birds to several hundred individuals. Along with the goldfinches, Pine Siskins will visit thistle feeders all winter long, and in a short time a large flock of these little gluttons can easily empty every thistle feeder in sight. The two species are easily separable in the field, siskins being heavily streaked with brownish-black above and below and having a longitudinal yellow wing stripe and yellow patches in the tail. The siskin also has a more tapered and slender bill which appears more pointed than that of the American Goldfinch.

There are a few nesting records for this species in Indiana, one of which occurred at the Indianapolis Museum of Art grounds after the famous winter of 1978. They nest early for a passerine, in April or early May, and both adults and young disappear shortly afterward, apparently moving farther northward for the remainder of the summer. The nest is usually placed twenty to thirty feet up in a conifer and is constructed of small twigs and pine needles. Four eggs to a nest is the normal clutch. Natural foods utilized by Pine Siskins range from grass seeds, thistle seeds, and sweet gum seeds to sycamore seeds. All of these food items have fairly thin exterior shells that are easily removed.

AMERICAN GOLDFINCH

Carduelis tristis

Habitat: Open fields interspersed with trees both deciduous and coniferous. Railroad rights-of-way, fencerows, and agricultural areas with extensive weed growth.

Local Sites: A familiar bird in suburban areas, where it comes readily to thistle feeders.

Status: Common summer resident. Breeds. Some years it remains throughout the winter with numbers augmented by more northern birds; other years they may be scarce.

Length: 5 inches.

Remarks: Before the advent of thistle feeders this attractive "wild canary," as it is often called, was a rare bird during the winter in the Indianapolis region. Now it is one of the more frequently seen birds at feeding stations. Although many consider it a permanent resident, most birds seen in winter are those which come to us from farther north, not our summer birds, which in turn have retired southward. We banded a female bird at Southport, Indiana, on 12 February 1972 that was recovered at Alpina, Michigan, on 6 May 1972 and then subsequently recovered once again near Pine Hills Nature Preserve on 15 February 1973, thus proving that at least this bird was strictly a winter visitor in our area.

Goldfinches are pugnacious to their own kind at thistle feeders, chasing and wing posturing each other, sometimes engaging in a mock battle where some feathers may occasionally fly and in general not tolerating close proximity to one another. They are nevertheless an attractive addition to our environs, exhibiting a variety of plumages as the seasons change. During the winter the birds are a muted olive-gray, while later in the year, as spring approaches, touches of bright yellow appear. Male birds reach a pinnacle of dazzling yellowness with jet black wings and crown patch during May.

Their nesting coincides with the maturing thistles, which appear in late July or in early August—too late for encroachments by the Brown-headed Cowbird. The nest, usually built in the fork of small twigs some two to thirty feet from the ground, is a neat little cup of finely woven vegetable fibers lined with thistledown. Here the female lays four to six pale bluish eggs while the male bird tends to feeding her during the twelve-to-fourteen-day incubation period.

EVENING GROSBEAK

Coccothraustes vespertinus

Habitat: Mixed coniferous-deciduous forests and city parks.
Local Sites: Eagle Creek Park, Holliday Park. Visits feeders during the winter but rather sporadically.
Status: Erratic winter visitor, usually rare. Appearing in late October and remaining in some areas until the first week of May.
Length: 8 inches.
Remarks: Arguably the most beautiful of the finches, Evening Grosbeaks are cyclical in occurrence in central Indiana with their appearance here depending upon the abundance of the food supply farther north. It is a gregarious bird, seldom seen alone—you see either none or medium to large groups, particularly around feeders which feature oil sunflower seed. They can rapidly decimate the seed supply at a station before departing in search of greener pastures. The bright yellow brow, underparts, and mantle, brown throat, nape, and crown, and black and white wings of the males are startlingly brilliant against a backdrop of snow. The plumage of the females is more subtle—shades of tan, gray, black, and white—but equally appealing. As you might surmise from the name, this species has a heavily built beak for cracking open seed husks. Frequently they are heard well before they are spotted, uttering a loud "tuuu-tuuu" as they fly from tree to tree in an undulating fashion with rapid wingbeats. As is typical of grosbeaks they are stockily built and rather short winged in appearance.

Evening Grosbeaks feed on some of the following naturally occurring foods: box elder seeds, beech nuts, hawthorn berries, and bittersweet berries, all easily planted as ornamentals in your yard. In the winter, if you should happen to attract some grosbeaks to your feeder, be sure to keep a good supply of seed out at all times, as they quickly depart when the food runs out.

HOUSE SPARROW

Passer domesticus

Habitat: Both urban and suburban areas near human habitation or in farm lots.
Local Sites: A familiar bird nearly everywhere.
Status: Common resident. Breeds.
Length: 6¼ inches.
Remarks: Just east of the downtown area of Indianapolis, near the 2600 block of Michigan Street, stood an old two-story house whose sideboards and shingles bore testimony to better times. Here, one of us used to watch House Sparrows build their nests in the downspout on the west corner. The nests were marvelous large, straw-like domed masses made up of a conglomeration of dried grasses, papers, and feathers. Each spring whenever there was a torrential downpour, the nest and its contents would wash through the downspout onto the splashblock below, and one could examine the soaked interior of this oven-shaped mass more closely. To the young onlooker the four greenish-speckled eggs inside were as precious as rare jewels.

The House Sparrow is technically a weaver finch, not a true sparrow. It was formerly known as the English Sparrow because the first birds were imported to this country from England. From this initial introduction in 1850 at Brooklyn, New York, and subsequent releases in Cleveland, Cincinnati, and Louisville, the bird proliferated throughout the North American continent, down the long arm of Central America, and into the continent of South America. It is unquestionably one of the most numerous birds in the world. Amos W. Butler wrote in 1898: "In 1871 and 1872, several hundred were brought to Indianapolis from New York City."

Ornithologists soon began to notice some of the destructive capabilities of the birds. They competed with the more beneficial species by usurping their nesting sites, destroyed fruits and vegetables, constructed dirty, sloppy nests, and in general made themselves public nuisances.

In southern Marion County, before they converted Greenwood Shopping Center into an enclosed mall, a sizable roost was located on the east side of L. S. Ayres. Here each evening, just before dark, hundreds of the birds would congregate in some decorative trees. When you walked nearby they would flush from the trees and cling to the side of the building in much the same manner as Chimney Swifts in a chimney. Flights of birds coming into the roost followed a more or less predicted direction.

Regardless of how you may feel about this dirty little ruffian, the House Sparrow is here to stay.

Suggestions for Further Reading

FEEDING AND ATTRACTING BIRDS

Adler, Jr., B. (1988). *Outwitting Squirrels*. Chicago Review Press.
DeGraaf, R., and M. Witman (1979). *Trees, Shrubs and Vines for Attracting Birds*. University of Massachusetts Press.
Dennis, J. V. (1986). *Beyond the Bird Feeder*. Alfred A. Knopf.
Dennis, J. V. (1976). *A Complete Guide to Bird Feeding*. Alfred A. Knopf.
Dennis, J. V. (1988). *Summer Bird Feeding*. Audubon Workshop, Inc.
Dobson, C. (1981). *Feeding Wild Birds in Winter*. Firefly Books.
Kress, S. W. (1985). *The Audubon Society Guide to Attracting Birds*. Charles Scribner's Sons.
McElroy, T. P. (1975). *The New Handbook of Attracting Birds*. Alfred A. Knopf.
Pistorius, A. (1981). *The Country Journal Book of Birding and Bird Attracting*. W. W. Norton and Co.
Schutz, W. (1974). *How to Attract, House and Feed Birds*. Collier Books.
Stokes, D., and L. Stokes (1987). *The Bird Feeder Book*. Little, Brown.
Terres, J. K. (1977). *Songbirds in Your Garden*. Hawthorne Books, Inc.
Waldon, B. (1991). *A Guide to Feeding Winter Birds*. Voyageur Press.

FIELD GUIDES

Chandler, R. J. (1989). *Field Guide to North Atlantic Shorebirds*. Facts on File, Inc.
Clark, W. S. and B. K. Wheeler (1987). *A Field Guide to Hawks of North America*. Houghton Mifflin Co.
Dunne, P., D. Sibley and C. Sutton (1988). *Hawks in Flight*. Houghton Mifflin Co.
Harrison, P. (1983). *Seabirds—an identification Guide*. Houghton Mifflin Co.
Hayman, P., J. Marchant, and T. Prater (1986). *Shorebirds—an identification Guide*. Houghton Mifflin Co.
Kaufmann, K. (1990). *A Field Guide to Advanced Birding*. Houghton Mifflin Co.
Madge, S. and H. Burn (1988). *Waterfowl—an identification Guide*. Houghton Mifflin Co.
Peterson, R. T. (1980). *A Field Guide to the Birds (East of the Rockies)* (fourth edition). Houghton Mifflin Co.
Robbins, C. S., B. Bruun, and H. S. Zim (1983). *A Guide to Field Identification—Birds of North America* (second edition). Golden.

Scott, Shirley L. et al. (1987). *Field Guide to the Birds of North America* (second edition). National Geographic Society.

OPTICS

Armstrong, A. (1990). *Binoculars for Birders*. Avian Press.
Robinson, L. J. (1989). *Outdoor Optics*. Lyons & Burford.

REGIONAL

Keller, C. E., T. C. Keller, and S. A. Keller (1986). *Indiana Birds and Their Haunts* (second edition). Indiana University Press.
Mumford, R. E., and C. E. Keller (1984). *Birds of Indiana*. Indiana University Press.

REFERENCE

American Ornithologists' Union (1983). *Check-list of North American Birds* (6th edition).
Bent, A. C. (1919–1968). *Life Histories of North American Birds*. Originally published by United States National Museum and Smithsonian Institution Press as a series of bulletins. Reprinted by Dover Publications (an illustrated edition is planned by Indiana University Press).
Freethy, R. (1990). *Secrets of Birdlife.* Blandford.
Ehrlich, P. R., D. S. Dobkin, and D. Wheye (1988). *The Birder's Handbook.* Simon & Schuster.
Farrand, Jr., J., ed. (1983). *The Audubon Society Master Guide to Birding* (3 volumes). Alfred A. Knopf.
Palmer, R. S., ed. (1962–). *Handbook of North American Birds* (5 volumes published, more to follow). Yale University Press.
Reader's Digest Association (1990). *Book of North American Birds.*
Stokes, D., and L. Stokes (1979–1989). *A Guide to Bird Behavior* (3 volumes). Little, Brown.
Terres, J. K. (1980). *The Audubon Society Encyclopedia of North American Birds.* Alfred A. Knopf.

Checklist of the Birds of the Indianapolis Region

The following checklist was originally published in the *Indiana Audubon Quarterly,* vol. 70 (1), February 1992.

Legend: C = common migrant/visitor, U = uncommon migrant/visitor, R = rare migrant/visitor, VR = very rare migrant/visitor, Acc = accidental, (n) = nesting, PR = permanent resident, H = hypothetical (physical proof lacking for Indiana or area), EX = exotic (escaped bird), X = extirpated (no longer found in area).

Loon, Red-throated .... VR____
    Pacific .... Acc____
    Common ....U____
Grebe, Pied-billed ....CM (n)____
    Horned...U____
    Red-necked .... Acc____
    Eared .... Acc____
    Western .... Acc____
Storm-Petrel, Band-rumped .... Acc____
Pelican, American White .... Acc____
    Brown... Acc____
Cormorant, Double-crested...............................U____
Anhinga .... H____
Frigatebird, Magnificent .... H____
Bittern, American ....R____
    Least...U (n)____
Heron, Great Blue ....C (n)____
Egret, Great...U____
Egret, Snowy... VR____
Heron, Little Blue...U____
    Tricolored... Acc____
Egret, Cattle.. VR____

Heron, Green-backed ....C (n)__
    Black-crowned Night- ....R__
    Yellow-crowned Night- .... VR__
Ibis, White .... Acc__
    Glossy.. Acc__
    White-faced.. Acc__
Stork, Wood.. Acc__
Whistling-Duck, Fulvous .... Acc__
Swan, Tundra ....R__
    Trumpeter... Acc__
    Mute ....R__
Goose, Greater White-fronted .... VR__
    Snow ....R__
Brant.. H__
Goose, Canada ....C (n)__
Shelduck, Ruddy..EX__
Duck, Wood...C (n)__
Teal, Green-winged .... C__
Duck, American Black.....................................C (n)__
Mallard..C (n)__
Pintail, Northern ....U__
Teal, Blue-winged...C (n)__
Shoveler, Northern .... C__
Gadwall .... C__
Wigeon, Eurasian .... Acc__
    American .... C__
Canvasback ....R__
Redhead .... C__
Duck, Ring-necked .... C__
Scaup, Greater... VR__
    Lesser .... C__
Duck, Harlequin .... Acc__
Oldsquaw .... VR__
Scoter, Black .... Acc__
    Surf... Acc__
    White-winged.. VR__
Goldeneye, Common... C__
    Barrow's .... H__
Bufflehead.. C__
Merganser, Hooded... C__
    Common ....U__
    Red-breasted .... C__
Duck, Ruddy..U__
Vulture, Black .... Acc__
    Turkey ....C (n)__

Osprey .... U___

Kite, Mississippi .... Acc___

Eagle, Bald .... R___

Harrier, Northern .... R (n)___

Hawk, Sharp-shinned .... U (n)___

Hawk, Cooper's .... U (n)___

Goshawk, Northern .... VR___

Hawk, Red-shouldered .... R___

    Broad-winged .... U (n)___

    Red-tailed .... PR (n)___

    Ferruginous .... H___

    Rough-legged .... U___

Eagle, Golden .... Acc___

Kestrel, American .... C (n)___

Merlin .... VR___

Falcon, Peregrine .... R___

Partridge, Gray .... X___

Chukar .... X___

Pheasant, Ring-necked .... PR (n)___

Grouse, Ruffed .... PR (n)___

Prairie-Chicken, Greater .... X___

Turkey, Wild .... PR (n)___

Bobwhite, Northern .... PR (n)___

Rail, Yellow .... Acc___

    Black .... Acc___

    King .... R (n)___

    Virginia .... R (n)___

Sora .... C (n)___

Moorhen, Common .... U (n)___

Coot, American .... C (n)___

Crane, Sandhill .... U___

    Whooping .... H___

Plover, Black-bellied .... R___

    Leser Golden- .... R___

    Semipalmated .... U___

    Piping .... Acc___

Killdeer .... C (n)___

Avocet, American .... Acc___

Yellowlegs, Greater .... U___

    Lesser .... C___

Sandpiper, Solitary .... C___

Willet .... VR___

Sandpiper, Spotted .... C (n)___

    Upland .... R (n)___

Godwit, Hudsonian .... Acc___

    Marbled .... Acc___

Turnstone, Ruddy .... R___

Knot, Red.. R___

Sanderling.. R___

Sandpiper, Semipalmated .... C___

    Western .... R___

    Least... C___

    White-rumped... R___

    Baird's .... R___

    Pectoral .... C___

Dunlin .... U___

Sandpiper, Stilt... R___

    Buff-breasted .... R___

Ruff... H___

Dowitcher, Short-billed .... U___

    Long-billed... VR___

Snipe, Common .... C___

Woodcock, American ....C (n)___

Phalarope, Wilson's .... R___

    Red-necked .... VR___

Jaeger, Pomarine .... Acc___

Gull, Laughing .... Acc___

    Franklin's .... VR___

    Bonaparte's .... U___

    Ring-billed.. C___

    California .... Acc___

    Herring... U___

    Iceland.. H___

    Glaucous .... Acc___

    Great Black-backed .... H___

Kittiwake, Black-legged .... Acc___

Tern, Caspian .... U___

    Common .... U___

    Forster's.. C___

    Least.. VR___

    Black .... U___

Murre, Thick-billed .... Acc___

Dove, Rock .... PR (n)___

    Ringed Turtle-.. EX___

    Mourning...PR (n)___

    Common Ground-.. Acc___

Parakeet, Monk .... EX___

Cuckoo, Black-billed .... C___

    Yellow-billed ....C (n)___

Owl, Barn... PR (n)___
    Eastern Screech-.. PR (n)___
    Great Horned... PR (n)___
    Snowy... VR___
    Burrowing.. Acc___
    Barred.. PR (n)___
    Long-eared.. R___
    Short-eared... R___
    Northern Saw-whet.. VR___
Nighthawk, Common...C (n)___
Chuck-will's-widow... Acc___
Whip-poor-will... R___
Swift, Chimney..C (n)___
Hummingbird, Ruby-throated.............................C (n)___
    Rufous... H___
Kingfisher, Belted ....C (n)___
Woodpecker, Red-headed ....C (n)___
    Red-bellied...C (n)___
Sapsucker, Yellow-bellied ....U___
Woodpecker, Downy.. PR (n)___
    Hairy .... PR (n)___
Flicker, Northern ....C___
Woodpecker, Pileated .... PR (n)___
Flycatcher, Olive-sided .... VR___
Wood-Pewee, Eastern..C (n)___
Flycatcher, Yellow-bellied..R___
    Acadian ....U (n)___
    Alder .... Acc___
    Willow...C (n)___
    Least ....C___
Phoebe, Eastern ....C (n)___
Flycatcher, Great Crested ....C (n)___
Kingbird, Western .... Acc___
    Eastern ....C (n)___
Flycatcher, Scissor-tailed .... Acc___
Lark, Horned..C (n)___
Martin, Purple ....C (n)___
Swallow, Tree ....C (n)___
    Northern Rough-winged.................................C (n)___
    Bank ....U (n)___
    Cliff..U (n)___
    Barn...C (n)___
Jay, Blue ....C (n)___
Magpie, Black-billed .... H___

Crow, American .... PR (n)___
Raven, Common ....X___
Chickadee, Black-capped .... Acc___
    Carolina... PR (n)___
Titmouse, Tufted .... PR (n)___
Nuthatch, Red-breasted ....U (n)___
    White-breasted.. PR (n)___
Creeper, Brown .... C___
Wren, Carolina... PR (n)___
    Bewick's .... Acc (n)___
    House..C (n)___
    Winter ....U___
    Sedge ....U (n)___
    Marsh ....R (n)___
Kinglet, Golden-crowned.. C___
    Ruby-crowned .... C___
Gnatcatcher, Blue-gray ....C (n)___
Bluebird, Eastern ....C (n)___
Veery ....U (n)___
Thrush, Gray-cheeked ....U___
    Swainson's.. C___
    Hermit.. C___
    Wood..C (n)___
Robin, American...C (n)___
Thrush, Varied .... Acc___
Catbird, Gray ....C (n)___
Mockingbird, Northern ....C (n)___
Thrasher, Brown ....C (n)___
Pipit, American ....U___
Waxwing, Bohemian .... H___
    Cedar ....C (n)___
Shrike, Northern .... VR___
    Loggerhead...R (n)___
Starling, European.. PR (n)___
Vireo, White-eyed..C (n)___
    Bell's...R (n)___
    Solitary ....U___
    Yellow-throated ....U (n)___
    Warbling...C (n)___
    Philadelphia...R___
    Red-eyed ....C (n)___
Warbler, Bachman's .... H___
    Blue-winged ....C (n)___
    Golden-winged..R___

Tennessee .... C___
Orange-crowned .... R___
Nashville .... C___
Parula, Northern .... U___
Warbler, Yellow...C (n)___
Chestnut-sided .... C___
Magnolia .... C___
Cape May... C___
Black-throated Blue .... R___
Yellow-rumped.. C___
Black-throated Green .... C___
Blackburnian... C___
Yellow-throated .... C (n)___
Pine .... R___
Kirtland's... H___
Prairie .... U (n)___
Palm .... C___
Warbler, Bay-breasted...................................... C___
Blackpoll .... C___
Cerulean ....U (n)___
Black-and-White .... C___
Redstart, American ....C (n)___
Warbler, Prothonotary......................................U (n)___
Worm-eating..R (n)___
Swainson's .... H___
Ovenbird ....C (n)___
Waterthrush, Northern .... C___
Louisiana...U (n)___
Warbler, Kentucky ....U (n)___
Connecticut .... R___
Mourning... U___
MacGillivray's .... H___
Yellowthroat, Common .... C (n)___
Warbler, Hooded .... R (n)___
Wilson's .... U___
Canada .... U___
Chat, Yellow-breasted...................................... C (n)___
Tanager, Summer.. R (n)___
Scarlet..C (n)___
Western .... H___
Cardinal, Northern.. PR (n)___
Grosbeak, Rose-breasted.................................. C (n)___
Black-headed .... H___
Blue ....R (n)___

Bunting, Lazuli.. H___
    Indigo ....C (n)___
    Painted .... Acc___
Dickcissel ....U (n)___
Towhee, Rufous-sided ....C (n)___
Sparrow, Bachman's.. Acc___
    American Tree...................................... C___
    Chipping...C (n)___
    Clay-colored... Acc___
    Field ....C (n)___
    Vesper..U (n)___
    Lark .... VR___
Bunting, Lark .... Acc___
Sparrow, Savannah..C (n)___
    Grasshopper..U (n)___
    Henslow's..R (n)___
    Le Conte's.. VR___
    Sharp-tailed .... VR___
    Fox ....U___
    Song.. PR (n)___
    Lincoln's..R___
    Swamp ....C___
    White-throated ....C___
    White-crowned ....C___
    Harris' .... Acc___
Junco, Dark-eyed ....C___
Longspur, McCown's .... H___
Longspur, Lapland ....U___
    Smith's .... Acc___
Bunting, Snow...R___
Bobolink...C (n)___
Blackbird, Red-winged ....C (n)___
Meadowlark, Eastern ....C (n)___
    Western .... VR___
Blackbird, Yellow-headed .... Acc___
    Rusty ....U___
    Brewer's.. VR___
Grackle, Common ....C (n)___
Cowbird, Brown-headed ....C (n)___
Oriole, Orchard...C (n)___
    Northern..C (n)___
Brambling... Acc___
Grosbeak, Pine... H___
Finch, Purple...U___
    House .... PR (n)___

142

Crossbill, Red...R___
    White-winged..VR___
Redpoll, Common ....VR___
    Hoary.. Acc___
Siskin, Pine..C (n)___
Goldfinch, American...C (n)___
Grosbeak, Evening..R___
Sparrow, House .... PR (n)___

Index

CHARLES E. KELLER is co-author of *Birds of Indiana* and *Indiana Birds and Their Haunts,* editor of the *Indiana Audubon Quarterly,* and sub-regional editor of *American Birds.*

TIMOTHY C. KELLER is a photographer, co-author of *Indiana Birds and Their Haunts,* and has served as an officer and on the Board of Directors of the Indiana Audubon Society and the Amos W. Butler Audubon Society.

Editor: *Roberta Diehl*
Book and Jacket Designer: *Pamela Albert*
Production Coordinator: *Harriet Curry*
Typeface: *Sabon/Sabon display*
Compositor: *Weimer Graphics*
Printer: *Maple-Vail Book Manufacturing*
Color insert: *Four Color Imports, Ltd.*